Diana Bilezikian

Dear Diana ...

To The Groziers With Regards From Diana

Diana's Guide To Independent Living

For Adolescents and Young Adults With Different Learning Styles and Special Needs

Diana Bilezikian

Illustrations by Ian Sullivan

Foreword by
Michael Storz, President of Chapel Haven, Inc.

AAPC
PUBLISHING
P.O. Box 23173
Shawnee Mission, Kansas 66283-0173
www.aapcpublishing.net

©2014 AAPC Publishing
P.O. Box 23173
Shawnee Mission, Kansas 66283-0173
www.aapcpublishing.net

Publisher's Cataloging-in-Publication

Bilezikian, Diana.

Dear Diana : Diana's guide to independent living for adolescents and young adults with different learning styles and special needs / Diana Bilezikian ; fore word by Michael Storz. -- Shawnee Mission, Kan. : AAPC Publishing, c2014.

p. ; cm.

ISBN: 978-1-937473-92-1
LCCN: 2014932486
Includes index.
Summary: Using a "Dear Abby" approach, the author, a person with special needs, answers simple questions about daily living designed to help other individuals with special needs, including developmental disabilities, to live independently.--Publisher.
Contents: Life, consumer, and financial skills -- Communication and interpersonal skills -- Self-care and domestic living -- Getting around, employment, and community participation -- Stress management -- Taking charge, managing priorities and solving problems -- Safety and emergencies.

1. People with disabilities--Life skills guides. 2. Teenagers with disabilities--Life skills guides. 3. Young adults with disabilities--Life skills guides. 4. Living alone--Handbooks, manuals, etc. 5. Life skills--Study and teaching. 6. People with disabilities--Housing. I. Title. II. Title: Diana's guide to independent living.

HV1568 .B55 2014
362.4/04--dc23 1403

This book is designed in Helvetica Neue and AT Studio Script.

Illustrations by Ian Sullivan.

Printed in the United States of America.

Dedication

This book is written in sad and loving memory of my dearly beloved sister, Sara Ann Bilezikian (February 22, 1978-January 12, 2002). Although she was younger than me by five years, she was like a big sister to me because of my special needs, and she taught me many things. She always meant well, and we had a lot of fun together.
I miss you, Sara. I love you and I shall never forget you.
May the Lord who created you bless you and keep you always happy.

Acknowledgments

Special thanks to my cousin Nancy Barnett, who first suggested that I write this book. I could never have written this book without the support, encouragement, and editorial assistance of my parents, John and Sophie Bilezikian. Thanks also to my editor, Kirsten McBride, for her valuable assistance.

Diana Bilezikian
New Haven, CT
January 2014

Introduction

After graduating from Scarsdale High School in 1991, I had no idea what I wanted to do with my life. I had worked hard to get that far. All my life, I had special needs, including the need for training in social, life, and vocational skills, as well as speech. I did not learn in the traditional way, and was always in special education classes. So, for me, the high school diploma was a huge accomplishment, but I didn't know what to do next. I was living with my parents, but I wanted my own life, and I didn't know how to achieve it.

My parents suggested that I consider Chapel Haven, a program for young adults with special needs and learning differences. It took me several years to finally realize that they were right. I started there when I was 20, and I have been part of the Chapel Haven Community ever since. With help from Chapel Haven, I have accomplished a great deal in my quest for independence. Currently, I am living independently and working at a retail store. I also am involved in several Chapel Haven-sponsored activities.

After my counselor and parents helped me to set up my computer, printer, and e-mail in my apartment, I started sending e-mails to my relatives and friends, giving a complete rundown of my life and the skills I was learning at Chapel Haven. I often wrote that I thought other Chapel Haven clients could benefit from my experiences in acquiring skills of independent living. It was my cousin, Nancy Barnett, who first suggested, "Diana, I think that you could write a book about independent living since there are many young adults with special needs who could really benefit from it." And that's when I thought to myself, “Hey, that sounds like a great idea! Why not? What I have learned about independent living might be useful to others if I write it down.”

So, that’s what I have done. Most of my advice throughout this book will be given in the form of Dear Diana letters. In other cases, I simply give advice in a straightforward way. The book also contains examples of word usage. In English, words are sometimes used in ways that have a completely different meaning. These “idioms” can be fun but also cause confusion if taken literally.

Writing this book has been an adventure and much hard work, but it was worth it. I have tried to cover many situations, and I have tried to keep my words as clear as possible so that my readers can benefit from my experiences. I hope that many young adults with special needs are able to benefit from my book. If so, the work will have been worth it.

Let us begin. Onward to independent living …

Foreword

More than 13 years ago, I found myself making a move from New Jersey to Connecticut. In doing so, I applied for a position at a remarkable program designed to teach adults with social and developmental disabilities the skills needed for living an independent and productive life. I was inspired by the success stories of young men and women who had overcome their challenges of navigating the world with differing abilities and were now living lives not so different from my own. I was thrilled to be offered an entry-level position at Chapel Haven. Now, 13 years later, as president of this unique and wonderful organization, I am honored to have the privilege to write this foreword for a remarkable young woman, Diana Bilezikian, who graduated from the program and is living out her dreams.

Dear Diana … Diana's Guide to Independent Living is a must-read for parents, siblings, teachers, professional staff, or any young adult who is striving toward independence. Diana brings to light many of the unique challenges that are often overlooked when teaching independence. Through her creative and witty approach, she allows her readers to experience the world through the eyes of a person with a social and developmental disability and in the process brings awareness to the areas that both educators and students must focus on if we are to achieve the goals of teaching true independence.

A colleague once said to me, "To understand how to teach somebody with autism spectrum disorders, you must first put yourself in their shoes and see the world through their eyes." *Dear Diana … Diana's Guide to Independent Living* accomplishes this in such a creative way that it leaves you wanting more.

I congratulate Diana on a publication over 20 years in the making. Thirteen years ago, I watched Diana sitting at a concert on a town green with her notebook and pen in hand, diligently writing about her life experiences. The same Diana is visible today, be it having breakfast at a nearby restaurant or on the campus of Chapel Haven. Although her book is complete, she has not stopped writing about the lessons she is learning in life. *Dear Diana … Diana's Guide to Independent Living* has changed the way I approach teaching and working alongside adults with special needs. Thank you, Diana.

Michael Storz, BA, MBA
President, Chapel Haven, Inc.
www.chapelhaven.org

Table of Contents

Chapter 1: Life, Consumer, and Financial Skills

Life Skills

Life skills include all those things we need to know and do so that we can live independently without needing help all the time. In this section, I discuss many important life skills.

Dear Diana,

I have been so busy that I hardly ever seem to be able to get anything done. The day is almost over, and my apartment is still a mess. I have had no time to pay my bills or do my laundry, and there was a message from my dentist's office that I forgot my appointment. I have a lot of trouble being organized. Do you have any advice for me?

Signed,

Chaotic Charlie

Dear Charlie,

You need to get a calendar with enough room on each date to write doctors' appointments and other obligations. Every night, check your calendar to see what is on it for the next day. Even if there is nothing special scheduled, having a general plan for the day is a good idea. On the following page is an example of a typical day for me.

Time	**Activity**
7:00 - 7:30 AM	Shower/get dressed/make bed
7:30 - 8:00 AM	Breakfast/brush teeth/get ready for work
8:00 - 8:15 AM	Walk to bus stop/wait for bus
8:20 AM	Take Bus #1 to Bus #2
9:05 AM	Take Bus #2 to work
10:30 AM - 2:30 PM	Hours of work (lunch at work)
2:30 - 4:00 PM	Take bus back home, Bus #2 to Bus #1, Bus #1 to home
4:00 - 6:00 PM	Shop, do groceries, see counselor, stay home for service calls, etc.
6:00 - 7:00 PM	Dinnertime (prepare dinner or eat out)
7:00 - 9:30 PM	Evening activities (pay bills, hang out with friends, go to a movie, watch TV, attend a concert or sporting event, do household chores or e-mail, etc.)
10:00 PM	Get ready for bed – Decide on what to wear the next day – Set the alarm clock to wake up in time – Brush teeth – Read a book – Lights out!

Try making a plan like this for yourself, and get yourself a calendar. I hope this helps.

Signed,

Diana

⌘

Dear Diana,

I am about to be fired for being late to work again. This is the fifth time that I have overslept and missed my bus. By the time I get ready and take the next bus, I get to work late. Can you help me, please?

Signed,

Always-Late Linda

Dear Linda,

You need an alarm clock. Many of us have trouble waking up in the morning. Without alarm clocks, we would oversleep and miss out on important responsibilities that depend on being on time. Luckily, we have alarm clocks to help us wake up in a timely manner. They have special bells (alarms) that, when set, begin ringing at the time you need to wake up. Before going to bed at night, be sure to set the alarm clock for the time you have to get up in the morning. Leave enough time after the alarm goes off so that you can get ready to meet your responsibilities on time. Sometimes it can be tricky to set the alarm. If you are having difficulty, get somebody to help you.

Some alarm clocks have snooze buttons so that when the alarm rings, you can silence it by pushing the snooze button. Then the alarm goes silent, but a few minutes later, it goes off again. If you are going to use the snooze alarm, set your clock a bit earlier to take into account your snooze time.

For some of us, it is difficult to get up even with the snooze alarm. Here's an idea to make sure you get up when the alarm goes off. Place the alarm clock on top of your dresser, far enough away from the bed that you will HAVE TO get up in order to shut it off. Once you have gotten up to shut the alarm clock off, don't go back to bed!

If you have a cell phone, it probably has an alarm, so you may want to use that. Be sure that it works and that the battery is charged up enough to last until morning.

Signed,

Diana

Making Good Use of the Newspaper

The newspaper is great for staying up on the news and the weather. You can also get the latest news and weather on your computer. But it's always good to have a newspaper to read on the bus or in a waiting room. Besides getting the news and weather, you can use the newspaper for other kinds of information. Here are some examples. (Always use the current newspaper. If the newspaper is a week old, recycle it, or use it to wrap up garbage.)

Dear Diana,

In which section of the newspaper can I look for an apartment?

Signed,

Carol

Dear Carol,

Look in the Classified section regarding apartments – be sure the newspaper is current.

Signed,

Diana

⌘

Dear Diana,

In which section of the newspaper can I look for a job?

Signed,

Mike

Dear Mike,

Look in the Help Wanted section regarding jobs using a current newspaper.

Signed,

Diana

Telephone Skills

The telephone is used for many purposes, including conversations with those whom we feel close to. You can learn more about how to use the phone in the examples below.

Dear Diana,

My cell phone battery is recharging, and my landline has a lot of static noise and doesn't seem to be working well. What should I do if I need to make phone calls?

Signed,

Bernice

Dear Bernice,

You can make phone calls from your cell phone even when it is charging. That should solve your problem for the moment.

However, if your landline continues to have static activity, you might have to call the phone company.

Signed,

Diana

⌘

Dear Diana,

I do okay calling my mother or my friends, but if I have to call a business or a doctor's office, I get nervous. It doesn't help that I have a speech impairment. Do you have any suggestions?

Signed,

Nervous Nellie

Dear Nellie,

Making business calls can be stressful. If you need to make one, it is useful to practice with somebody first. Write everything down on a piece of paper ahead of time. For example, if you want to order checks from the bank, write down your name, home address, phone number, and account number. Practice reading this to a person on the other end of the line. Pretend to be using a phone and speak smoothly with appropriate volume. Start the call by saying, "Hello. I would like to order more checks, please."

You can use the same technique to order pizza! If the message is written down ahead of time and you practice, you won't get so nervous. Another alternative is to use your computer and the Internet and send written messages instead. Try it, and good luck.

Signed,

Diana

Dear Diana,

In the bus, there is a sign saying, "Keep your cell phone conversations private by speaking quietly." I have trouble speaking quietly because of my speech impairment, but sometimes I need to let my roommate know that I'm on my way home. What can I do?

Signed,

Cell Phone Cindy

Dear Cindy,

Text messaging is a good way to use your mobile phone if you're on the bus or in some public place where it would annoy others if you talked. If your phone has a vibrating option, you can keep it on, but set it so that instead of ringing, it just vibrates, in case somebody is trying to text you.

Signed,

Diana

Making Collect Calls

Sometimes you may have to make a collect call, but remember that when you do, the person who accepts the call will be responsible for the charges. You might have to call collect if your cell phone is not working and you don't have money to make the call using a public payphone. Pick up the receiver of the phone, listen for the dial tone, dial "0" for operator, and then the 10-digit number that you want to call. Now, listen for a tone followed by recorded instructions about making a collect call. Speak your name when prompted. Alternatively, talk directly to an operator by dialing "0." Tell the operator that you need help in making a collect call. If you must use a payphone, hang onto your pocketbook or wallet, keep an eye on your bags, and be aware of the people around you. Because there are so many cell phones now, payphones are becoming hard to find. If you need to make a collect call and can't locate a payphone, it is perfectly acceptable to ask a friend if you could use his or her cell phone to make the call.

Computers and the Internet

Computers are useful. In addition to using computers to write messages and reports, you can count on the computer – via the Internet – to give you information about the news, weather, websites, and much more. If you have never used a computer, you need to get somebody to teach you or take a computer course. It is also a good idea to get somebody to help you hook up the computer and set up an e-mail account.

E-mail is a wonderful way to stay in touch with people. Whenever you log onto the Internet, you will find all sorts of ads and pop-ups inviting you to "click here" for this and that. Never click onto anything unfamiliar. Delete it. Never open e-mail from strangers. Delete those e-mails.

Dear Diana,

The other day I got the strangest e-mail. The person who wrote it said his name was Joe. He was writing as though he knew me, but I'm not sure who he is. Anyway, he wrote he was on vacation and that his wallet had been stolen. He said if I would just send him a thousand dollars, he would pay me back double when he finally got home. That's a lot of money, and I'm pretty sure I don't know him, but on the other hand, I feel sorry for him. What do you think I should do?

Signed,

Mary

Dear Mary,

This is why you should never open e-mails from unknown senders. Joe is what's called a scam artist. He's trying to fool you into sending him money. If you do, you will never see the money again, and you will never see Joe. Delete his e-mail and do nothing else.

Signed,

Diana

⌘

Dear Diana,

I got an e-mail from somebody whom I don't know. He said his name was George and he wanted to be my e-mail friend. He asked me to write back and send him a picture of myself. I didn't do that, because I haven't figured out how to send pictures. Then George asked me for my address and said he'd like to meet me for coffee. He sounds so nice. What do you think?

Signed,

E-Mail Pal Emily

Dear Emily,

This is an example of how dangerous the Internet can be. Don't send George your address, and under no circumstances give him your last name. Don't meet him for coffee. Don't write to him any more. If he sends you any more e-mails, delete them before you open them. You have no idea who this person is. For all you know, he could be a serial killer, a sex offender, or dangerous in some other way. Only correspond on the Internet with people you know.

Signed,

Diana

⌘

Dear Diana,

I have read in the newspapers about awful situations where mean girls get together and gang up on someone by sending insulting and nasty comments by the Internet. I read about a case where the girl getting these e-mail messages got so upset that she tried to kill herself. I hear that this can also happen on Facebook! Can you give me advice about this?

Signed,

Worried Wendy

Dear Wendy,

What you wrote to me about is called "cyberbullying." It is totally unacceptable behavior and becoming a huge problem, especially among teenage girls. It is a lesson for all of us. Never send nasty e-mails, by yourself or in a group, to anyone. If you do, you would be cyberbullying. If you receive such a note, by e-mail or on Facebook, go immediately to your counselor, parents, or an adult whom you trust. Ask them what to do.

Signed,

Diana

Tipping

A tip is money that you give to somebody who has provided service to you and who has been nice and friendly. For example, you typically tip beauty parlor people, hotel staff, taxi drivers, pizza delivery people, and servers in restaurants. In general, tip 15-20 percent. For a 15 percent tip, multiply the bill by .15. For example, if it costs $13, multiply by .15 for $1.95 as the tip. In that case, round it up to $2. You might find it helpful to carry a tip card in your wallet, especially if you get flustered trying to do math. You can usually buy a tip card at a newsstand or gift shop.

Dear Diana,

I was short on money when I took a cab home the other day and decided not to tip the cab driver, even though he was very nice. He gave me no trouble about it, but I wonder if maybe it might have been a good idea to tip him anyway?

Signed,

John

Dear John,

It is always a good idea to tip cab drivers unless they are extremely unpleasant. From now on, be sure to budget enough money for tipping whenever you take a cab. Tip at least 15 fifteen percent of the fare.

Good luck!

Signed,

Diana

Consumer Skills

Being a good consumer ensures that you get the things that you need at the best price. It involves social skills as well as problem solving.

Grocery Shopping

Dear Diana,

I went to the grocery store for milk. It is a huge store and they sell everything. So, I decided to purchase Hawaiian Punch™, cupcakes, cookies, chicken, sausages, and much more, except I forgot the milk. So, now, my roommate Jack is pissed at me. He has a point that I really did screw up. Do you have any advice for me?

Signed,

Impulsive Ira

Dear Ira,

That's the problem with these big supermarkets. Sometimes you end up buying everything you see. Always check what you already have at home and make a list of items to buy before going to the grocery store. When you get there, stick to your list and don't go buying a lot of stuff that you didn't write down and don't need, no matter how tempting it seems.

Better luck next time.

Signed,

Diana

Dry Cleaning

Dear Diana,

At home, my mother always took care of all the laundry, but now I'm on my own and I don't know where to begin. I put one of my favorite sweaters in the washing machine and dryer, and it shrank so much that I can't wear it any more. Should I have taken it to the dry cleaners instead? How do people figure out what to do?

Signed,

Careless Carrie

Dear Carrie,

Oh, dear! I'm so sorry. You have learned the hard way that you must read the care labels on the garment. Every bit of clothing in your closet, including your underwear, will have a label telling you how to get it clean. If the item is machine-washable, it will say so, and it will usually even tell you what water temperature to use. If the item is not to be put in the dryer, it will say that as well. Sometimes the label says "Dry clean only." In that case, don't put the garment in the washing machine. Take it to the dry cleaners.

Signed,

Diana

⌘

Dear Diana,

I have some pants that need to be shortened. I called my mother to see if she could do it, but she said to take them to the dry cleaners. I don't understand. I haven't even worn the pants yet and they aren't dirty. Why did she say that?

Signed,

Confused Clyde

Dear Clyde,

If you need a garment professionally altered, dry cleaners often have somebody who can do that for you. If you see a sign in the window that says "ALTERATIONS," then you are all set. You have to try the pants on at home and decide how many inches you would like to have them shortened. If you aren't sure, sometimes the store has a little private dressing area where you can put the pants on and let them help you decide. I recommend doing that at the store if you possibly can.

Whenever you leave something at the dry cleaners for any service, it is a good idea to find out how much they will charge, because that is exactly how much you will have to pay when going to pick it up. Instead of asking your mother about this, now you can take care of it yourself. And, your mother will be very proud of you for this example of living independently.

Good luck!

Signed,

Diana

Gift Cards

Gift cards are popular. If someone gives you one, be careful not to lose it, because it is worth the same as cash. Below are some tips for using gift cards.

Dear Diana,

I just received a gift card from my grandmother for 50 dollars at my favorite clothing store. I've been looking at a sweater in the window of the store. I don't know if the sweater costs 50 dollars – or more or less. What should I do?

Signed,

Karen

Dear Karen,

Take the gift card with you, go into the store, and find out how much the sweater costs. Suppose the sweater costs 35 dollars. The gift card is worth 50 dollars. If you want to pay for the sweater with the gift card, they will take the card and deduct 35 dollars plus the sales tax. They will return your gift card to you, because it will be worth 50 dollars minus what you ended up paying for the sweater. It will also say on your receipt that the gift card still has money left. Hang onto the gift card. You can use the balance in the future.

Signed,

Diana

⌘

Dear Diana,

Okay, I went to the store again a week later and I saw a pocketbook for 20 dollars, but my gift card is only worth 12 dollars. Now what happens?

Signed,

Karen

Dear Karen,

If you want the pocketbook, you can pay for it with your gift card plus an additional 8 dollars plus tax by cash or check. You don't have to do the math. They will swipe your gift card in their computer and tell you exactly what you have to pay. If you use the gift card for this purchase, you have used up all the money in the gift card and you should throw it away.

Signed,

Diana

Pharmacies

Most people buy their toiletries, such as shampoo and conditioner, toothpaste, etc., at the pharmacy, because you can usually get a better deal on such items there than at the grocery store. Many pharmacy chains issue a special card to use when you shop that will give you an even better deal.

If you need a prescription filled, go to the special window where the registered pharmacist will fill it for you. Sometimes, they can fill it right away. If not, they will tell you when to come back. If you have a prescription plan as part of your health insurance, be sure to tell the pharmacist.

Clothes Shopping

Like shopping for anything, when you are shopping for clothes, it is best to get only what you need. Sometimes, if you are looking for something for a special occasion, it is a good idea to shop with a friend whose opinion you can trust. Before you pay for anything, be sure that you understand whether or not the item is returnable or exchangeable if you change your mind and are not satisfied with it. Sometimes when things are on sale, they cannot be returned for a refund.

Dear Diana,

I just bought a dress for a really fantastic price – half off the original price. When I got home and tried it on one more time, I didn't like it so much after all. I took it back to the store, but the saleswoman showed me that on the price tag it said FINAL SALE and, therefore, she was unable to refund my money. I don't understand. Can you please explain this to me?

Signed,

Barbara

Dear Barbara,

Before you pay for anything that's on sale, be sure to ask whether or not it is returnable. The store will tell you before they take your money. If the price tag says FINAL SALE, you don't even need to ask. Just be sure you really want the item before you leave the store, because you cannot return it. So, now you understand. Better luck next time.

Signed,

Diana

The Post Office

The post office is a part of the United States Postal Service. At the post office, you may mail packages or regular mail, pick up packages or regular mail, and buy stamps.

You will need stamps whenever you want to mail letters or postcards. If you don't put a stamp on your letter or postcard, it will be returned to you if you have provided a return address. You need to know what the postage rate is, because it changes often. It is helpful to have a supply of stamps on hand so that you don't have to go to the post office every time you need to mail a letter or postcard.

Some people prefer to have mailboxes in the post office. If you are a mailbox holder at the post office, you will have a key that opens the box and lets you collect your mail. Remember that if you want a mailbox at the post office, you will have to pay a fee. Otherwise, the mail carriers come by to deliver your mail, leaving it either underneath your doorstep, in a mail slot, or in a locked mailbox that is close to your apartment. If the mail carrier delivers the mail to a mailbox in a central location close to your apartment, there is no charge.

Dear Diana,

I came home from work and there's a yellow slip in my mailbox that says PACKAGE with a return address from my favorite aunt, but there's no package. What should I do?

Signed,

Person Missing Package

Dear Person Missing Package,

The postal service doesn't like to leave packages outside your door, because they might get rained on or stolen. Hang on to the yellow slip. Take it to the post office and give it to the clerk at the window. He or she will give you your package.

Signed,

Diana

Dear Diana,

I mailed a thank you note to my grandmother for the present that she sent me, but today it came back in my mail. There was a message stamped on the envelope that said: "RETURNED FOR POSTAGE." Now, what should I do?

Signed,

Phoebe.

Dear Phoebe,

Look at the envelope. Did you forget to put a stamp on it? If so, cross out the note that says "RETURNED FOR POSTAGE," put a stamp on it, and put it back in the mailbox. It's a good thing you gave them your return address, because otherwise you never would have known what happened to the letter.

Signed,

Diana

Financial Skills

We all need to understand how to manage our money whether or not we have paying jobs. The following guidelines will help you to manage your finances properly.

Budgeting Systems

Dear Diana,

Because I love coffee mugs, I bought three new ones for my collection as soon as I took my weekly allowance out of the bank. I also bought a few sweatshirts. I don't really need them, but they were on sale and I liked them. But, now I have no money left for my groceries. I don't even have enough money for the bus tomorrow. This happens almost every week. I'm always running out of money. My counselor says that this shouldn't be happening. What can I do?

Signed,

Moneyless Mike

Dear Mike,

One budgeting system that has worked for me and that might work for you too consists of using envelopes marked for specific purposes. The envelopes would contain money to cover your expenses for a given week. One envelope might be marked "toiletries," and in that envelope, you would put enough money for whatever toiletries you need that week, like shampoo or toothpaste. Another envelope could be marked "public transportation," and in that envelope, you would put enough money for bus fare for the whole week. Other categories for which you would have an envelope with an appropriate amount of money include weekly entertainment (movies, bowling, etc.), groceries, clothes, and other expenses. My system also has an envelope for emergencies. You should always have money saved and immediately available for an emergency. It doesn't help if your money is in the bank when the emergency occurs. Never spend your emergency money on sweatshirts or mugs, even though they are on sale. I suggest you talk this over with a counselor, parent, or other trusted individual.

Signed,

Diana

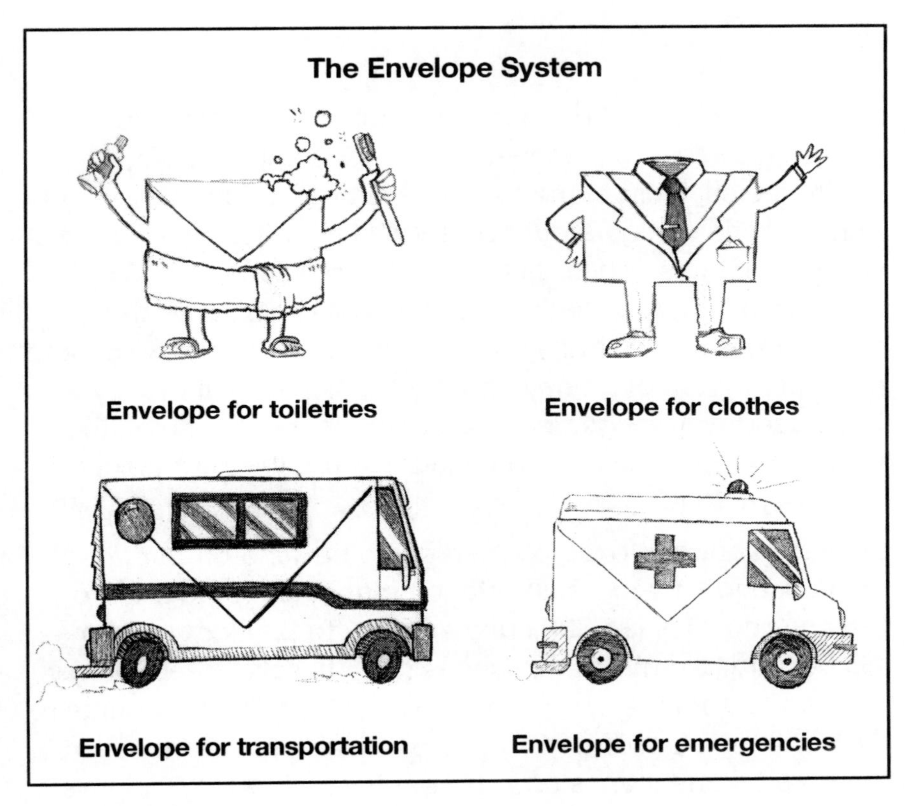

Dear Diana,

Thank you for your advice about the envelope system for budgeting my money. I have envelopes now, but I need more help with how this system really works. Can you give me more help?

Signed,

Mike, the Envelope Man

Dear Mike,

Here is my system. For each envelope, I write what it is for: transportation, groceries, toiletries, entertainment, emergencies, etc. Let me explain even more. For transportation, I figure out how much I need for the bus every week. In my case, the bus fare is 65 cents each way ($1.30 round trip) 5 days a week. This amounts to $6.50 for the entire week. On the transportation envelope, I write $6.50 and put that amount of money into the envelope. That money is to be used only for getting to and from work. I write on the other envelopes how much I need and put the right amount of money into it.

Let's take another example, like going bowling on Saturday with a friend. I need transportation money to get to and from the bowling alley ($1.30). I need money to pay for two games ($5.00) and to rent bowling shoes ($2.50). I also need money for a soda from the vending machine ($1.50). This amounts to $10.30 for my bowling trip. I place that amount of money in my entertainment envelope and don't use it for anything else. I do this for all my envelopes.

I hope the envelope system will work for you.

Signed,

Diana

⌘

Dear Diana,

Thanks so much for this neat envelope system. I went to the bank to take out the amount of money that I need to fill all my envelopes. It was $100. The bank teller gave me five $20 bills. I can't fill my envelopes because I don't have the exact amount of money for each. What did I do wrong?

Signed,

Mike, Getting the Hang of It But Not Quite There Yet

Dear Mike,

If you need $100 to fill your envelopes for the week, you would have to withdraw $100 as your weekly allowance. Make sure that the denominations of the bills allow you to put the proper amount of money into your envelopes. For example, if you have allocated $5 for your public transportation envelope, be sure that you have either a $5 bill or five singles. For your groceries envelope, you will need two $20 bills. Before you go to the bank, write down how many singles, fives, tens, and twenties you want. Make sure it adds up to one hundred. Take this list with you when you go up to the teller's window.

I think you will find that this system works for you as it does for me!

Signed,

Diana

Deposits, Checking and Savings Accounts

Dear Diana,

I'm new in town, and I've just opened a checking account at the bank. But I don't exactly understand how to use it. How do I put money in and how do I take money out?

Signed,

Billy

Dear Billy,

Your checking account is intended for the money that you will withdraw from the bank as cash or write a check from if you are shopping or paying bills. You need to keep enough money in your checking account for your regular needs. If you have more money than you need in your checking account, it should go into your savings account where it will earn interest.

Money can be deposited into your checking account by a check made out to you ("Pay to the order of Billy ….______") or you can deposit cash into your checking account. You need to fill out a deposit slip with the amount of money you are depositing. Deposit slips are either in your checkbook or at the bank. Your account number is already on the deposit slips if they are from your checkbook. If you get them from the bank, you must write your account number on them. Your account number is also on your checks.

Sometimes, money will be deposited directly into your checking account; for example, if you receive any state or federal benefits, they are often deposited directly into your account. You need to look at your account statement to see when this has been done. If the money is there, you can use it for groceries or other needs.

Signed,

Diana

Sources of Income: Job, Social Security, and Other Sources

Dear Diana,

I get paid from my job every other week. Because of my disability, I also receive payments from other sources, like the state government and the U.S. government. It is confusing to have several different payments. How would you suggest that I keep track of this?

Signed,

Violet

Dear Violet,

Good question! It's important to know what your sources of income are. From your job, you need to know how much you will be paid, how often, and when. If you have a disability, you may be getting additional money, such as SSI, which stands for Social Security Supplemental Income. This will be deposited directly into your checking account. With your counselor, social worker, or parents, you can make a list of how much money you are receiving from these and possibly other sources every month. This way, you will know what your monthly income is.

Signed,

Diana

⌘

Dear Diana,

I'm concerned because my paycheck isn't enough to cover my bills. I haven't seen my benefits coordinator in six months. What should I do?

Signed,

Concerned

Dear Concerned,

First, you need to get somebody, a parent or a qualified counselor, to sit down with you and review your budget. You may be eligible for federal and state benefits that will help you pay your bills. On the other hand, maybe you are spending money on things you don't need. The envelope system I mentioned earlier will help you ensure that you have enough money on necessities, such as rent, utilities, food, and transportation.

Good luck!

Signed,

Diana

⌘

Dear Diana,

I have carefully checked my income with my counselor. It comes from my job and benefits. I'm using the envelope system. But I still don't have enough money at the end of the month to pay my bills. What should I do?

Signed,

Wilson

Dear Wilson,

This is indeed a problem, and you have to do something about it. You might want to get an apartment mate to share the rent with or see if you can work more hours at your job. I suggest contacting your life skills counselor, who can help you deal with this problem.

Good luck!

Signed,

Diana

⌘

Dear Diana,

I'm doing some volunteer work, but I need a job that pays so that I can pay my rent, my bills, and buy groceries. I am not sure who to contact to help me.

Signed,

Sally

Dear Sally,

Most adult programs have vocational counseling services. If you are in such a program, somebody there will help you. The vocational counselor will be able to check the Help Wanted ads with you and will have other ideas. Another possibility is to talk to the person in charge of your volunteer program to see if they have any leads. That person may also be able to write you a letter of recommendation, which may help you get a paying job. Finally, if you have family or friends who are working for pay, ask them to ask their boss if more workers are needed.

Good luck!

Signed,

Diana

⌘

Dear Diana,

I have a habit of letting my mail pile up day after day after day. When my father came to visit, he looked in the pile and noticed that I had a bill from the phone company, which should have been paid two weeks ago. He reminded me that if I don't pay my phone bills on time, I will have to pay penalties and they might cut off my phone. How should I deal with this problem?

Signed,

John

Dear John,

It is a good idea to check your mail every day. Look at every piece of mail. Sometimes your mail contains important information, like bills that have to be paid, along with junk mail. I suggest that you place your important mail in a separate pile to be dealt with and throw away your junk mail. That way, your mail won't pile up, and you will have identified important mail to be dealt with now. If you need help in the beginning, be sure to ask a parent or other trusted adult.

Signed,

Diana

⌘

Dear Diana,

I get bills every month from the telephone company and the cable company. I pay the bills by check and place the check along with the return statement in the return envelope. I put a stamp on the envelope, seal it, and mail it. Part of the bill does not get returned with my payment. What do I do with it?

Signed,

Lisa

Dear Lisa,

It is a good idea to save the part of the bill showing how much you paid in a folder so you will know that you paid the bill. Have a different folder for each company. For example, one for the telephone company, one for the cable company, and so on. Some people like to store their folders in a desk drawer or file cabinet. After a year, you can throw the statements away if your counselor says it's okay.

Signed,

Diana

Chapter 2: Communication and Interpersonal Skills

Language

The English language can be confusing, because it is full of idiomatic expressions. If you run into an idiomatic expression, and take it literally, you will not understand its meaning. I am going to give you a few examples in this chapter. There are hundreds of expressions in English. Watch for more throughout the rest of the book.

Dear Diana,

What does the expression "Draw a line in the sand" mean?

Signed,

Line Inquirer

Dear Line Inquirer,

The expression "Draw a line in the sand" doesn't mean literally drawing a line in the sand with a stick or other instrument. This expression is used when two people confront each other over an issue about which they don't agree. For example, John says to Mary, "I'll cook dinner, but I refuse to wash the dishes," or Mary says to John, "If you insist, I'll take your mother shopping, but I refuse to go to Filene's Basement."

Signed,

Diana

Dear Diana,

My friend Jane said that she didn't have time to talk to me, because she had to "catch a bus." I'm confused. How was she going to do that? A bus is much too big to catch with your hands.

Signed,

Karen

Dear Karen,

When we use the expression "catch a bus," we mean that we will be at the bus stop when the bus arrives so that we can board it. It's just an expression. Don't try to catch the bus with your bare hands or by any other means.

Signed,

Diana

Catching the Bus.

Catching the bus: wrong! **Catching the bus: right!**

Dear Diana,

What does the expression "Sit here for the present" mean?

Signed,

Present Wonderer

Dear Present Wonderer,

That expression does not mean that you're going to get a present if you sit there. It means "Come sit here for now." The word "present" in this case means "right now." It does not refer to a gift.

Signed,

Diana

Dear Diana,

What is the meaning of the term "monkey business"?

Signed,

Curious About Monkey Business

Dear Curious About Monkey Business,

The expression "monkey business" is used to describe activities that are foolish or nonsensical. Hiding your sister's hair barrettes in her slippers just to be mischievous would be an example of monkey business.

Signed,

Diana

Dear Diana,

What does the expression "Curiosity killed the cat" mean?

Signed,

Sarah

Dear Sarah,

Cats are naturally curious, and it can get them into trouble. For example, let's say a lady had to shoo her cat out of the living room because it got too interested in her ball of knitting wool and made a huge mess of it. Sometimes people get in trouble for being curious, too. In social situations, for instance, don't ask somebody how much he weighs or what color his underpants are. Those are personal questions and, therefore, none of your business. If you are on the receiving end of a personal question, you don't have to answer it. Just smile and say, "Curiosity killed the cat."

Signed,

Diana

Curiosity Killed the Cat.

The cat is getting curious!

The cat got too curious!

Dear Diana,

What does the expression "down to the wire" mean?

Signed,

Wire Inquirer

Dear Wire Inquirer,

"Down to the wire" means waiting until the very last minute to get things done. When we say that we don't want to get "down to the wire," we mean that we don't want to procrastinate. It is always a good idea to do things ahead of time so that we will not be down to the wire.

Signed,

Diana

Dear Diana,

What does the expression "You're making a mountain out of a mole hill" mean?

Signed,

Wondering About a Mole Hill

Dear Wondering About a Mole Hill,

"You're making a mountain out of a mole hill" means that you're making a big problem out of a little problem instead of coming up with some solutions on how to deal with it. For example, you got everything on your mother's grocery list, except you forgot the mustard, and now your mother is

making a big fuss. She is "making a mountain out of a mole hill" by fussing over one little thing when you remembered everything else.

Signed,

Diana

Dear Diana,

What does the expression "Let's cross that bridge when we come to it" mean?

Signed,

Bridge Crosser

Dear Bridge Crosser,

The expression "Let's cross that bridge when we come to it" means let's worry or deal with the issue when the time comes, not before. For example, your sister complains that celebrating Christmas with your cousins is so stressful that she doesn't want to do it, but your brother disagrees, insisting that you invite them. Finally, your mom says, "Look, why don't we cross that bridge when we come to it? It's not even close to Christmastime. It's only July. There's no point in discussing it now."

Signed,

Diana

Dear Diana,

What does the expression "Don't count your chickens before they hatch" mean?

Signed,
Chicken Person

Dear Chicken Person,

Just because a hen lays six eggs doesn't mean you're going to get six chickens. One or two of the eggs may crack ahead of time or the chicken inside may not live to be hatched. The expression "Don't count your chickens before they hatch" means "Don't count on it" or "Don't get your hopes up until it really happens." Suppose you are in a program for independent living and you think that you are ready to live alone without apartment mates, but you don't have a job yet that will allow you to pay for the rent on a place of your own. Your mother advises, "Don't count your chickens before they hatch." She then explains "I wouldn't get my hopes up if I were you for it can be expensive to live by yourself. It might be a good idea to have at least one apartment mate to share the expenses with until you are ready for this next step in your independence."

Signed,

Diana

Interpersonal Skills and Appropriate Behavior

Appropriate behavior and good interpersonal skills are critical, because they show consideration of other people. If we don't demonstrate appropriate behavior, we may be perceived as unfriendly, rude, inconsiderate, and otherwise off-putting. The following is a mix of "Dear Diana" questions and answers and more direct advice and suggestions. And as always, you'll be introduced to more idioms.

Dear Diana,

My Aunt Tillie couldn't come for Christmas this year, but she sent me a package with lots of nice things. Is it okay to send her an e-mail to thank her?

Signed,

Mary

Dear Mary,

E-mail is okay and certainly better than nothing, but if Aunt Tillie has taken the time to send you a nice package, it would be better to send her a handwritten thank-you note. Here is an example of what you could say:

> *December 27, 2013*
>
> *Dear Aunt Tillie,*
>
> *Thank you for the cool sweater. I love it. It's just what I wanted, and I really appreciate your thoughtfulness.*
>
> *I hope to see you soon.*
>
> *Thanks again.*
>
> *Love,*
>
> *Mary*

If you write this kind of thank-you note to Aunt Tillie, I know she will appreciate it. You can use this thank-you note as a guide to other thank-you notes.

Signed,

Diana

⌘

Dear Diana,

I am sick and tired of my parents constantly getting on my case about practically everything. "Clean up your room!" "Those pants are too tight!" "Eat your vegetables!" "Brush your teeth!" It drives me crazy. Do you have any advice for how to handle it?

Signed,

Cindy

Dear Cindy,

You need to tell your parents how you feel about this. In many cases, I'm sure that your parents are correct, but perhaps they can remind you in ways that are not so off-putting. Also, as you learn to live up to your responsibilities without being told, your parents won't be on your case as much.

Signed,

Diana

⌘

Dear Diana,

Michael and I are coworkers at a grocery store. We often work together and help each other out. One day his girlfriend, Lucy, was shopping in the store, and when she saw us, she got jealous and accused Michael of cheating on her, and now she isn't speaking to either one of us. What can I do?

Signed,

Kathy

Dear Kathy,

You and Michael need to sit down with Lucy and explain to her that your boss gives you jobs that require two people. This kind of situation can cause trouble, but I hope she will understand.

Signed,

Diana

⌘

Dear Diana,

In my office skills class, Counselor Carol told me to take some papers over to Counselor Barbara and ask her to staple them together. But when I did, Barbara told me I had to wait, because she was busy working with others. What can I do?

Signed,

Mary

Dear Mary,

Go back to Carol and tell her what Barbara told you. Then ask Carol for some more work to do while you're waiting.

Signed,

Diana

⌘

Dear Diana,

My friend Joe is obese. I have been joking around and making fun of him, and now he doesn't want to be my friend any more. But I'm just kidding. Don't you think he needs to learn to take a joke?

Signed,

Becky

Dear Becky,

It sounds like you are not laughing "with" Joe but "at" him, which is not appropriate. I'm not surprised that Joe doesn't want to be your friend any more. You owe him an apology. It is never appropriate to tease people because of their size, weight, speech impairment, baldness, or any other personal trait. You wouldn't like it if you were unique in some way and people made fun of you. So, don't make fun of others either.

Signed,

Diana

⌘

Dear Diana,

There are times when I yawn loudly and then break into a laugh. I think this is funny. But everybody tells me it's annoying. What do you think?

Signed,

Donna

Dear Donna,

It is annoying, and it isn't funny. Don't do it any more. In addition, it is rude and unhygienic to yawn, sneeze, cough, laugh, or talk loudly in other people's faces.

Signed,

Diana

⌘

Dear Diana,

Sometimes when I talk to somebody, I get too close and invade their personal space. Can you help me, please?

Signed,

Space Invader

Dear Space Invader,

You need to remember to keep a reasonable distance between yourself and others. An arm's length between you and the other person is generally considered a reasonable distance. Privately, try to see how much space that is so you don't actually measure the space when you are out in public.

Signed,

Diana

⌘

Dear Diana,

I put a fake plastic Halloween spider by my sister Katie's place at the dinner table. She got terribly frightened, assuming it was real. When I laughed, everybody told me it wasn't funny. But then I picked up the spider, shook it, laughed, and said, "I got you! I put it there as a joke! It's fake!" Now my dad says I'm "in the doghouse" and nobody appreciates my humor. I don't understand what he means – we don't even have a dog. What do you think?

Signed,

Norman

Dear Norman,

The doghouse is where you belong. That's an idiomatic expression that means you should be punished. I wouldn't be surprised if they sent you to your room. Practical jokes are not funny. They are also not always safe. I suggest that you revise your brand of humor so you don't scare or hurt people.

Signed,

Diana

P.S. Remember that the most important way of expressing humor is to do it safely and not at anybody's expense.

Norman "In the Dog House."

Norman in the dog house: literally.

What the expression really means: "Norman, you misbehaved. Go to your room!"

Dear Diana,

I sometimes fool my sister Irene to get her to come downstairs and not stay in her room all day. For instance, I tell her that some of her favorite famous people are visiting us (although they really aren't) as a trick to get her to come downstairs. She gets very excited and immediately comes running. But then she's like, "Well, where are they?" I giggle saying, "Got you, Irene! They're not here! It was just a trick to get you to come downstairs – fooled you!" She gets so angry that she stomps back upstairs to her room. I want her to come down and join the rest of the family, but I worry this is not the right way to do it. What do you suggest?

Signed,

Kerry

Dear Kerry,

It's not nice to fool people like that. Try to find out why Irene stays in her room all day. You could suggest that the two of you take a walk, go shopping, go to a movie, or play a game. These suggestions might make Irene feel better and want to come downstairs. This way, you respect her decision but also give her an opportunity to do something together.

Signed,

Diana

⌘

Dear Diana,

The other day I accidentally spilled my milk! Honest. It was an accident! But just the same, after wiping it up, I got sent to my room. What can I do?

Signed,

Sarah

Dear Sarah,

Parents or guardians sometimes make mistakes. After an episode like this, try settling down in your room for a while. After you have settled down, perhaps you will be better able to explain to your parents that it was an accident. If they understood that it was an accident, I don't think that they would have sent you to your room.

Signed,

Diana

⌘

Dear Diana,

As much as I love playing games with people, I hate it when I lose. What should I do when I lose?

Signed,

Gary

Dear Gary,

Nobody likes to lose, but you need to remember that it's only a game. It's important to be a good sport whether you win or lose.

Signed,

Diana

⌘

Dear Diana,

I am pregnant and due to have my first baby in six months. Suddenly, my friend Kathy doesn't want to be my friend any more. She says that babies take up a lot of time and energy. My feelings are really hurt. What can I do?

Signed,

Gracie

Dear Gracie,

Of course, it hurts. If I were you, I would explain to Kathy that you can still be friends even after the baby comes. Most mothers maintain friendships, and there is no reason why you and Kathy can't still be good friends. However, it won't be the same relationship after the baby comes. You and Kathy may not be able to go off shopping, out to lunch, etc., whenever you wish. But if Kathy is willing to come to your place, you can keep up your friendship. As the baby starts to grow up, there are more things that you can all do together such as going to the zoo or the park.

Signed,

Diana

⌘

Dear Diana,

I have not been nice to Mary, the new girl in school. In fact, a bunch of us have decided that we hate her. We don't play with her, and when she approaches us, we say, "Oh, no, here comes Mary, the jerk!" We got in trouble the other day for behaving like this, but when the teachers talked to us about the Golden Rule, I didn't know what they were talking about. Please help!

Signed,

Sarah

Dear Sarah,

The Golden Rule means treating others the way you would like to be treated yourself. It sounds like you need to stop copying inappropriate behaviors. You and your friends should think about how you would feel if somebody treated you the way you treat Mary. When Mary approaches, leave out the "Oh, no" and just say, "Here comes Mary." Saying "Oh, no!" isn't nice. And don't make fun of her, call her mean names, or say that you hate her. You don't even know her. How can you hate her? "Hate" is a very strong word. Try including her in your games. Who knows? She might turn out to be very nice. Learn to accept people as they are. Don't put them down just because they're different. Try to defend Mary by telling the others, "Stop being mean to Mary! She's my friend!"

Good luck!

Signed,

Diana

Interruptions

Interruptions can be tricky, because sometimes it is appropriate to interrupt and at other times it is not. You interrupt somebody when what you have to ask or tell them is important and, therefore, has to be taken care of right away. If you must interrupt, always remember to say, "Excuse me." Apologize for the interruption and explain that it was necessary to get the person's attention right away. Here are some questions and answers on this topic.

Dear Diana,

My dad was on the phone in his study on a conference call with coworkers in Europe the other evening. I was having a lot of trouble with my math homework, so I went into the study to ask him for help. He got angry and yelled at me. He knows perfectly well that math is hard for me and often helps me with it. What do you think?

Signed,

Luisa

Dear Luisa,

I'm not surprised that your dad got angry and yelled at you. It is perfectly OK to ask for help, but this was not an emergency. Your dad was on a long-distance conference call, and in such a case, unless you are dealing with a true emergency, interrupting him is inappropriate. Next time, wait until your dad is off the phone and then ask him if this is a good time for him to help you. If he says yes, then that's just fine. If no, ask him if he can help you later.

Signed,

Diana

⌘

Dear Diana,

I was in the grocery store the other day and I couldn't find any cooking oil. There didn't seem to be any grocery store people around, but I found somebody who was restocking the shelves in the aisle where they had detergents. I didn't want to bother him, because he seemed busy, but finally I asked him to help me. He told me to look in aisle 3 on the right. So, I went there and found what I needed. Did I do the right thing to interrupt him while he was doing his work?

Signed,

Sue

Dear Sue,

Yes, you absolutely did the right thing. Part of this person's job is to help customers. It is fine to say, "Excuse me, can you please tell me where the cooking oil is?" After all, if customers can't find what they are looking for and leave without buying anything, it won't be good for business.

Signed,

Diana

⌘

Dear Diana,

My teacher sent me down the hall to Mr. Brown's room to use his photocopier, but when I got there, the door to his classroom was closed and it sounded like he was busy conducting a class so I didn't interrupt. My teacher really needed the photocopying done, so I was worried that she would be annoyed when I came back empty-handed, but she wasn't. So, I guess I did the right thing, but I'm a little confused. What do you think?

Signed,

Peter

Dear Peter,

Yes, you did the right thing not to interrupt Mr. Brown when he was conducting a class, and your teacher understands that. I'm sure your teacher would never have sent you down the hall if she had known that Mr. Brown was busy conducting a class.

Signed,

Diana

⌘

Dear Diana,

Sometimes if I have a great idea and am all excited about it, I talk loudly and end up interrupting others around me who are trying to do their own work. They get irritated and tell me to "HUSH!" I don't like being spoken to that way. So what do you suggest I do?

Signed,

Bossed-Around Loud Person

Dear Bossed-Around Loud Person,

I understand how you feel. I don't like being spoken rudely to either. Nobody does. I'm sure that those you interrupted didn't mean to hush you up so rudely any more than you meant to disturb them with loud interruptions. First of all, everybody owes each other apologies. Second, you need to understand that the exact moment you have a great idea might not be the best time to barge in and interrupt. Wait for the appropriate time and place to tell people about it.

Good luck!

Signed,

Diana

⌘

Dear Diana,

My mother was on the phone talking to her best friend. Sometimes they go on for hours and hours, but I noticed that there was smoke coming out of the clothes dryer. So, I ran to get Mom. At first, she was annoyed, but then I told her that there was a fire. She hung up on her friend and immediately called the fire department. What will Mom's friend think?

Signed,

Charlotte

Dear Charlotte,

You absolutely and positively did the right thing, and so did your mom. After it's all over, surely, Mom will call back her friend to apologize and explain the whole story.

Signed,

Diana

Intrusions

Intrusive behavior doesn't necessarily involve breaking into somebody's place, spying on them, or reading their mail. It can just be a matter of words. For example, if your so-called friend wants to know how much you weigh or what medicines you take, she is being intrusive. It is also intrusive when your peers give you advice that you didn't ask for such as, "You should be on a diet." Only your doctor or other health professional should be giving you personal advice like that. Telemarketers frequently call trying to sell merchandise that you have not asked about or are interested in. These people are being intrusive, and you should hang up on them.

Dear Diana,

My sister Sarah keeps a journal. She writes in it every night, but during the day, I know it's hidden under her pillow. I was curious to see if she had written anything about me. So, once when she was out, I went into her room and read her journal. She didn't write anything about me, just about people who I don't even know, but still, I am feeling kind of bad about it. What do you think?

Signed,

Francesca

Dear Francesca,

You had no business sneaking into your sister's room and reading her journal even if you thought she was writing about you. It doesn't matter who she was writing about. Her journal is private and not any of your business. How would you like it if someone sneaked into your room and read your diary?

Signed,

Diana

⌘

Dear Diana,

I was going through a stressful period, so my doctor prescribed some tranquilizers. I have my own bathroom and I keep them in the medicine cabinet, but one day I came home from work early and found my roommate poking around in there. She said she was just looking for some aspirin, but then she asked me why I was taking tranquilizers. I was very upset with her and didn't know how to answer her. How do you think I should have responded?

Signed,

Polly

Dear Polly,

Your roommate was being very intrusive. I don't believe she was looking for aspirin, do you? You must tell her politely but firmly to stay out of your medicine cabinet. You might ask her how she would like it if you opened her medicine cabinet and found out what medications she was taking.

Signed,

Diana

⌘

The following section presents behaviors and situations and advice for how to demonstrate good social skills and appropriate behavior.

Being Passive, Assertive, Aggressive

Our behavior is often broken down in general categories: passive, assertive and aggressive. These behaviors are not in and of themselves inappropriate, but it is important to know their definition and use them when the situation calls for it.

Passive – Not taking action to do something. For example, you are afraid to tell somebody how you feel about the way they are treating you for fear that they will take it personally and probably decide not to be your friend any more. Don't be passive, but at the same time be tactful. If you express yourself tactfully, you can make your point without losing your friends.

Assertive – Being active and firm. For example, telling somebody firmly how you feel about a situation. Make sure that even an assertive statement is polite. For instance, "Listen,

Aunt Susan, I really appreciate your interest in my knitting, but I would prefer that you didn't stretch it, okay, please?" Hopefully, Aunt Susan will respond appropriately, saying something like, "Sure, no problem, Kathy. I'm so sorry."

Aggressive – Being overly assertive. Sometimes this can take the form of overreacting. For example, using the knitting example, saying something like, "Hey! Stop stretching my knitting or I'll punch you in the nose!" This kind of behavior is overreactive, aggressive, and even threatening. It is also completely unacceptable.

Jealousy

Sometimes jealousy stems from fear of losing the love of somebody you care about. Jealousy can also be envy of somebody who seems to be doing something better than you or who has something that you wish you had. If you are jealous, it helps to remember that you probably have something that somebody else wishes to have but doesn't have. Jealousy is not a nice or healthy feeling. Learn to accept things as they are. Just because your best friend has a new friend does not mean that he doesn't care about you any more.

Lying

Lying is saying something you know is not true. Therefore, it is not appropriate behavior. You are lying, for example, when you break a vase and make up a story that "the elephant did it." A "white lie" is a special type of lie that you say when you don't want to hurt somebody's feelings. Therefore, it is usually not considered inappropriate behavior. For example, pretend that you are visiting somebody and are offered an apple that you don't care for. Instead of saying, "Yuck! No!"

you can tell this white lie: "Oh, no, thank you. I just ate." Here's another example: Let's say somebody you know but don't really want to spend time with invites you to dinner. You could say, "I'm so sorry; I have another commitment that evening."

Gossip and Rumors

To gossip means to go around talking about other people's personal business behind their backs and spreading rumors about them. Here's an example. "Margaret, did you hear what Susan said to Tom about Mary!" Whether or not the rumors are true, this is not proper behavior. You wouldn't like it if people gossiped about you. Other people's private lives are none of your business and vice versa.

Giving Compliments

It is nice to compliment people for all kinds of reasons. Here are some examples.

"I love your dress, Constanza. You look so pretty in it."
"That's a nice tie, Clarence. It makes you look so handsome."
"Clara, you're doing a great job cleaning up."
"Cornelia, you sure knit beautifully."

Accepting Compliments

When you have received a compliment, it is polite and expected for you to respond by acknowledging the compliment. Here are some examples from the people who were complimented above.

Constanza (her nice dress): "Why, thank you, Millie, for your nice compliment about my dress. I truly appreciate it."
Clarence (his nice tie): "Gee, thanks, Millie. It is one of my favorite ties. It was a present from my grandmother."

Clara (cleaning up): "Thank you so much, Millie. Happy to help."
Cornelia (knitting): "Thanks so much, Millie. I love knitting."

Notice in all of these examples, the person being complimented says "Thank you" and adds a small other comment. If you can't think of something to add, you can just say, "Thank you."

Giving and Accepting Apologies

If you realize that you have acted badly towards a friend, it's important to make amends. Failure to do so can result in loss of friendship. Contact your friend and apologize. That usually is all that you need to do, because friends understand each other and don't need more than a simple apology before moving on.

"I'm sorry" is what you say when you have done or said something that bothers another person even if you didn't intend to. Here's an example: You are cleaning up the office and happen to throw out somebody's coffee thinking that they were finished with it, when, in fact, they weren't. They say, "Hey! I wasn't finished with my coffee yet!" So, you must say, "Oh, dear, I'm so sorry. I won't do it again."

If somebody has hurt your feelings or has been unkind to you, it is easy to hold a grudge. If the person expresses a sincere and genuine apology, the proper response is: "I accept your apology. And I forgive you." Try not to hold a grudge, and the next time you see the person, don't bring up that subject no matter how much you still remember it.

Dear Diana,

My dad has been helping me with my homework and also trying to understand when I might not need any help. It has been frustrating for both of us. When I apologized to him, he said it wasn't necessary. I am confused.

Signed,

Millie

Dear Millie,

I'm sure that what your dad meant was that it's silly to apologize when you didn't do anything wrong. You only apologize when there is a reason to apologize. It doesn't sound to me like you and your dad were arguing. Very good! Keep it up! So, don't waste time apologizing for no reason at all.

Signed,

Diana

⌘

Dear Diana,

I sneaked into my apartment mate John's room and took his pen the other day. It made him furious and he yelled at me, which made me cry. Now we are not speaking to each other. What should I do?

Signed,

Peter

Dear Peter,

The first thing you need to do is apologize to John. You have no right to go into his room and take his things, even if you were planning to return the pen. If you stop doing it, he'll probably stop yelling at you. Had John done that to you, you surely would have yelled at him. The two of you need to set rules and get along as apartment mates.

Signed,

Diana

Constructive Criticism

Constructive criticism is a special kind of a criticism that is not meant to insult but to help you to be better at things. This kind of criticism should primarily come from a parent, a teacher, a counselor, a physician, your boss, or a close friend or family member. For example, a mother compliments her daughter on her appearance, adding that she would be even more beautiful if she washed her hair more often. Sometimes we forget that the suggestions are meant to be helpful – constructive – and get hurt or angry. Here are four steps for learning how to deal with constructive criticism.

1. Remain calm. (Remember that the person is trying to help you to become a better person.)
2. Listen carefully. (If you don't understand the suggestion, ask questions.)
3. Thank the person nicely for the suggestion.
4. Consider following the suggestion for improvement.

Sympathy and Condolences

If you know somebody who has lost a friend or family member, send your condolences. You may write, e-mail, call, or speak to them in person, but don't ignore the situation by doing nothing, and don't wait too long to send sympathy and condolences. The sooner, the better. A condolence note does not have to be long or complicated as long as it expresses your feelings of sorrow. An example of a condolence note is:

> *Dear Sylvia,*
>
> *I am so sorry that you lost your mother.*
>
> *You are in my thoughts.*
>
> *Sincerely,*
>
> *Jack*

When to Talk and When to Keep Quiet

This is an important distinction, because it is not proper to talk when we are not supposed to, nor is it proper not to talk when we are supposed to. That is, we don't talk when others are talking. But if it's your turn to say something and you don't say something, that isn't proper either. Here is an example:

Peter is talking: "Jack, I have had the most exciting weekend. I went with my father on a camping trip … What did you do this weekend?"

At this point, Jack should respond by telling Peter what he did, like, "Peter, my father and I went shopping for a television set …" If Jack did not respond when Peter asked the question, that would have been inappropriate.

Ignoring People

To ignore means to pay no attention to somebody or something. Sometimes it is appropriate to ignore and at other times it is not. For example, if somebody is making fun of you, it's best to ignore them. Also, if a stranger in a public place tries to strike up a conversation with you, ignore them and walk away if you possibly can. On the other hand, if your counselor asks you to do something, or if your friend greets you, you should respond.

Acceptable Socializing

One of the greatest challenges for adults with different learning styles is to socialize in an acceptable way. Sometimes, we are too sociable and at other times, we are not sociable enough. The challenge is to strike the right balance. Here is an example of acceptable socializing: You are at a party. You sit next to somebody who is knitting.

1. Compliment the person on how beautiful the knitting project looks, praising her for her talent and asking her how she learned to knit so beautifully.
2. Ask your party friend what she is making and whom it's for.
3. Don't touch the knitting project and never stretch it.
4. Refrain from making suggestions about how the knitting project might be improved, unless you are asked.

I have just given you an example of proper socialization behavior. Now, let me give you a list of dos and don'ts.

Inappropriate Questions

Never ask personal questions such as the following in public:

1. "What color underwear do you wear?"
2. "How much did you pay for that sweater?"
3. "How much do you weigh?"
4. "At your doctor's appointment, what did you discuss?"
5. "How come you broke up with your lover?"
6. "Tell me about your private phone conversations."
7. "How much money do you have in your pocketbook?"
8. "I heard that you got grounded. How come?"
9. "What were you discussing privately with that other person you were talking to?"
10. You are in charge of answering the phone. Somebody calls to say that they have great news for your boss. You ask the caller, "What is the great news?"
11. You ask your friend if he or she got any interesting personal mail.
12. "Did you have sex with your lover?"

Appropriate Questions

The following list consists of examples of questions that are appropriate to ask in public:

1. "What kinds of music do you like?"
2. "Do you have a job?"
3. "What do you like to do in your spare time?"
4. "What's your favorite food?"
5. "Do you have any brothers or sisters?"

6. "Do you have any pets?"
7. "What's your favorite TV show?"
8. "Do you like baseball?"
9. "Do you like to go shopping?"
10. "What do you do on your job?"
11. "What's your favorite season?"
12. "Do you text?"

Waiting in Line

When lining up at the movie theater, the post office, etc., the line always starts at the end. Get behind the last person in the line. Don't cut in front of people who are in line. Don't worry; the line will move, and before you know it, you will have moved up to the front.

Reasons for Saying, "Excuse Me"

It is appropriate to say, "Excuse me" in many situations. For example, it helps to explain behavior that could be taken the wrong way. If you fail to say, "Excuse me" in such situations, your actions could be interpreted as rude, clumsy, or otherwise inappropriate. Here are some examples of when saying "Excuse me" is definitely indicated:

1. When you burp, even if accidentally
2. After you cough
3. When bumping somebody by accident
4. When you want to get past somebody
5. When you must appropriately interrupt somebody
6. When you have to leave a discussion momentarily because the phone is ringing

Monopolizing

Don't monopolize the conversation. Don't talk just about yourself. Occasionally, ask others what's new with them and be sure to speak with appropriate volume and speech. Suppose you are out walking and see some of your neighbors coming toward you. Stop briefly and say hello, but don't stop for a long chat, because they probably have plans, and so do you.

Another example is seeing an acquaintance at the bank, the grocery store, or the doctor's office. It is perfectly acceptable to say "Hello, how are you?" and then go on about your business. This way, you have acknowledged the person, but you have not taken up her time.

Table Manners

Having a meal with somebody, like a friend or family member, is an important aspect of socialization. It follows then that eating should be associated with proper table manners. Here are some guidelines:

1. Come to the table on time, well groomed, and dressed appropriately.
2. Sit down when everybody else is ready to sit down.
3. Grace might be said or sung. You should feel free to join in. If you feel uncomfortable, simply stand or sit and wait until grace is over.
4. Participate in passing the serving plates around so that everybody has a chance to take some food from every plate.
5. Only put on your plate what you can reasonably eat. Don't pile your plate with food.

6. Don't start eating until everybody has been served and your host/hostess has begun.
7. If you have not been offered a plate of food, don't reach across the table for it. Politely ask, "Please pass the peas." Then say, "Thank you," when they are passed to you.
8. Always have a napkin in your lap and use it on your hands or face when necessary.
9. Take little bites, one at a time. Don't gorge your mouth with large amounts of food. This can be gross, disgusting, rude, and dangerous.
10. Chew with your mouth closed.
11. Don't talk with your mouth full. It is not only rude, but you might choke that way. Swallow what you are eating before you speak. If somebody asks you a question while you have food in your mouth, point one finger up meaning, "Wait a minute." Proceed to answer the question after you have swallowed your food.
12. Eat slowly.
13. If you need to use the bathroom during the meal, politely say, "Excuse me for just a minute. I'll be right back." Everybody will understand.
14. Don't hunch over your food. Sit up straight.
15. Never lick plates, cups, or silverware. That's gross.
16. If there is bread in the bread basket and it is passed to you, you can pick up a piece of bread with your fingers. If there is a bread tong, use that to pick up your piece of bread.

17. You can use your hands for certain foods like corn on the cob, sandwiches, etc. For other things, use utensils. If there is any doubt about how food should be eaten, do what your host/hostess does.
18. When you are done, put your utensils in the center of the plate; and don't push your plate away.
19. When you are all finished, wait until everybody else is finished. It is rude to leave the table before everybody else is finished.
20. Thank the host/hostess for dinner.
21. After the meal, offer to help clean up.

How to End a Phone Call

You are having a phone conversation with somebody you know, but you feel it's time to end the conversation; besides, you have to go out. It would be rude to just hang up or to slam the phone down. Instead, politely say, "I have to go now. It was great talking to you. I hope you have a good day tomorrow and we'll talk again soon." Typically, the other person will say, "Thanks. The same to you. Take care," and then you both politely hang up.

Being on Time

There are many situations in which you are expected to be on time, such as getting to work, being picked up by somebody, or meeting somebody for coffee. Don't make people wait for you. If you are delayed for any reason, call the person and say you will be late, and be sure to apologize when you arrive.

Staring at People

It is never appropriate to stare at people, particularly if they happen to look funny, talk funny, act funny, have physical handicaps, are very tall or short, fat or thin, wear glasses, are bald, wear hearing aids, crutches, or helmets, or need wheelchairs. These situations must be appreciated and respected. When people are stared at for any of these conditions, it makes them feel uncomfortable and self-conscious. If you find yourself staring, ask yourself how you would like it if you were being stared at. That should stop you.

When to Wish Somebody Good Luck

"Good luck" is a phrase that we use a lot. It is meant to wish somebody the best and can be used in many situations. For example, if somebody is going to take a test, wishing them good luck is appropriate because you are hoping that they will pass the test. Suppose your friend is being interviewed for a new job, it is appropriate to wish her good luck because you hope that she will get the job.

When to Send Somebody a Get-Well Message

Most of the time it is not necessary to comment when somebody has a minor sniffle, cough, or runny nose. But sometimes the illness is more serious such as the flu, pneumonia, heatstroke, splitting headache, earache, etc. In these situations, it is appropriate to call the person and wish him or her a speedy recovery. If the person has been sick and perhaps has been in the hospital, you might want to send him a get-well card. Alternatively, you can send your get-well message by e-mail. Unless the person wants to talk to you about the details of his illness, it is not appropriate for you to ask.

Startling People

When you are close to people and they are not expecting a sudden voice or movement, they often get startled. Startling is always upsetting. So, remember that if you're going to call or shout out to somebody who is nearby, you may startle them. Nevertheless, through no fault of yours, somebody could be startled and if that happens, be sure to apologize.

Speaking Clearly With Appropriate Volume

When speaking, it is important to do so clearly in a voice that is neither too loud nor too soft. If your voice is too loud or too soft, the listener may tell you, and then it is your job to adjust your own volume so that it is appropriate.

Responding Properly to an Invitation

If you get an invitation to a party in the mail, you must respond promptly and let them know whether or not you can attend. The person who is planning the party needs to know who is coming, so it is rude not to answer. If you cannot come, it is not necessary to give the reason why but simply to politely say, "Thank you for inviting me. I'm so sorry I cannot join you. I'm sure the party will be great."

Congratulating Somebody

When somebody does something well, it's polite to congratulate the person. When somebody receives an honor, such as a high school diploma, it is also appropriate to give congratulations. There are many other situations when congratulations are in order, such as passing a test, getting a job, getting married, having a baby, etc. The proper phrase for congratulating somebody is, for instance, "Congratulations, Mary! I heard that you just got a new job. I'm so proud of you. Tell me about it."

Congratulating somebody is a sign that you care about the person and are happy for the good news.

Borrowing Other People's Things

Occasionally, you may be in need of something that you don't have but would like to borrow, like a calculator. Ask, "May I borrow your calculator?" Also, tell the person who lends you the item when you will return it, and then make sure you do. If you don't return it by the time you promised, the lender may not let you borrow anything again. Of course, while you are using it, treat it with respect and never damage it. Finally, be sure to say "Thank you" when you return the borrowed item.

Eavesdropping

To eavesdrop means to listen in on private conversations, whether this occurs by phone, by listening from behind a closed door, or from another room. When you are not invited to participate in a conversation, you should not be involved. Eavesdropping is always inappropriate. Don't do it.

Taking Advantage of People

Some people take advantage of others by asking them for favors, for money, for help with laundry, shopping, etc. This is unacceptable behavior if it happens too often because friendships are built upon respecting others and not making them feel put upon. When you take advantage of people, they eventually begin to resent you, and you may lose their friendship. When friends help each other, on the other hand, they are not taking advantage of each other because they are helping each other. Friends, by definition, don't take advantage of each other.

Gestures and Body Language

Many mannerisms are never appropriate, such as sticking your tongue out at somebody, making funny faces, giving somebody the finger, or holding your nose. These gestures are offensive and indicate lack of respect for others. If you don't particularly like somebody, never express yourself that way.

Abusive or Profane Language

Never use abusive or profane words. If you want to use a nasty word, instead, say something like, "Oh, dear!" or "Shoot!" Be careful not to call somebody a "retard," a "jerk," or "stupid." These are hurtful terms.

When Meeting New People

If you're introduced to somebody at a party, school, or workplace, respect the person's personal space, make eye contact, and use a firm handshake. Say, "How do you do? I'm pleased to meet you." When the conversation is over, say, "It was a pleasure meeting you."

When to Say, "You're Welcome"

"You're welcome" is a polite phrase used after you have done something nice for somebody and they thank you for it. For example, upon being thanked after helping somebody carry in the groceries, say "You're welcome. It was my pleasure. I will be happy to help you any time."

Keeping Certain Things Private

Here are some things that you should not do in public: Make out with your lover, fuss with your clothes, talk loudly on your cell phone, change or breastfeed a baby. (If you must nurse or change a baby, do it as discreetly as possible and in a way that does not offend other people.) If you are with friends in a public place, don't discuss personal things with them where others might hear. When you see your doctor, counselor, or other professional, keep your conversations with them private.

Rules for Hosts and Guests

Being the Host/Hostess:

1. Be sure to clean up your place well in advance of the party/visit.
2. Make sure you have enough drinks and refreshments on hand.
3. When you are expecting guests, be sure you are at home to greet them.
4. When they arrive, greet your guests and ask them how they are.
5. Lead them into your place. Hold the door open politely.
6. Offer to take their coats.
7. If your guests are staying overnight, take them to the guest bedroom where they can leave their suitcases.
8. Offer them a tour of your place.
9. If your visitors compliment you on how beautiful your place looks, accept it graciously.
10. Offer them a seat before serving drinks and refreshments.
11. Don't be insulted if they don't finish what you have served. They may not be hungry.

12. Try not to be on the phone while you have guests, unless it's an emergency. Let your answering machine pick up calls. Deal with your messages after they leave.
13. Maintain a pleasant conversation.
14. Don't expect guests to bring gifts. But if they do, be sure to thank them for their thoughtfulness.
15. If you want to listen to music, be sure to choose music that your guests can also enjoy. (No earphones.)
16. When you guests thank you for your hospitality, politely say, "You're welcome."

Being the Guest:

1. Don't help yourself to drinks and refreshments. Don't ask for them. Wait until they are offered to you.
2. If you are offered something that you don't care for, simply say, "No, thank you, but thank you for offering."
3. If a plate of food is served to you, taste some of it and be polite. Remember that you need not finish it, but you must always be polite.
4. Don't snoop in your host's/hostess' room or on their computer. Do not read their mail.
5. Say something nice about your host's/hostess' place.
6. If you are spending the night, it is nice to bring some flowers or a small gift.
7. When leaving, be sure to say "Thank you."

Conduct at a Live Performance

1. Focus your attention on the stage.
2. Keep quiet during the performance. Don't whisper to your seatmates and be sure that your cell phone is turned off.
3. When the performance is over, clap and applaud.
4. If you get to meet the performers afterwards, give them your compliments in person. Sometimes it's a good idea to ask them where they learned to perform so well.
5. At the end of the performance, file out of the auditorium in an orderly manner.

That was some section! Let's take a break and discuss a few idiomatic expressions. As you remember, idiomatic expressions are not supposed to be taken literally.

Dear Diana,

What does the expression "We don't have to stop cold turkey" mean?

Signed,

Cold Turkey Person

Dear Cold Turkey Person,

The expression "We don't have to stop cold turkey" means that we don't have to stop completely and immediately, but gradually. For example, you have been meeting with your counselor twice a week for a while. You are doing so well that you think you would like to stop the sessions immediately. Your counselor advises you that rather than stopping immediately, you start to taper them off. For example, your sessions could be once a week instead of twice a week. This is an example of "not stopping cold turkey." This expression is often used when somebody tries to stop drinking or smoking abruptly.

Signed,

Diana

Dear Diana,

What does the expression "I'm beginning to smell a rat around here" mean?

Signed,

Bewildered Bella

Dear Bella,

The expression "I'm beginning to smell a rat around here" means that you are suspicious that something is not quite right. For example, you reach into your pocketbook for money to pay for your groceries and realize that your money is gone. You remember that earlier that day your friend asked to borrow a quarter and you answered, "Oh, sure, just take one out of my pocketbook." Now you're wondering if your so-called friend took the rest of your money as well. This is a bad situation. In this situation, it is appropriate to say, "Gee, I'm beginning to smell a rat around here."

Signed,

Diana

Dear Diana,

What does the expression "Kill two birds with one stone" mean?

Signed,

Bird Person

Dear Bird Person,

The expression "Kill two birds with one stone" means doing two things at the same time. Let's say that you plan to go out to mail some letters and pick up milk at the grocery store on the same errand. You could be said to "Kill two birds with one stone" by taking care of both errands on the same trip.

Signed,

Diana

Killing Two Birds With One Stone.

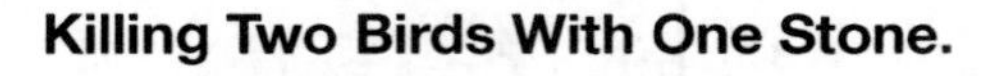

"Killing two birds with one stone" is shown literally above.

But the real meaning of this idiomatic expression is "doing two things at the same time, as seen in the man above, who is both reading and exercising!

Dear Diana,

What does the expression "Speaking of the devil" mean?

Signed,

Bedeviled

Dear Bedeviled,

The expression "Speaking of the devil" does not mean that you are speaking about the devil. The word "devil" in this phrase is not a bad word, nor does it imply that the people whom you are referring to are devils. It means that you are speaking about somebody and that he or she shows up all of a sudden. For example, Mary and John are talking about their friends Sarah and Steven, who appear all of a sudden. Mary says, "Well! Speaking of the devil!" What she really means is "The very people we were just talking about have suddenly appeared!"

Signed,

Diana

Dear Diana,

What does the expression "Give somebody a taste of their own medicine" mean?

Signed,

Medicine Man

Dear Medicine Man,

Let me give you an example of what this expression means. Let's say that James is always late for dates with his friends. He doesn't care about how they feel about it and doesn't stop to think about how he would feel if somebody treated him that way. One day, Kathy says, "Let's give James a taste of his own medicine. Let's see how he likes it when we are late." So all his friends are late and make him wait. James doesn't like it any better than they did when he was late. So, now he has received a taste of his own medicine. Clearly, this expression has nothing to do with medicine but relates to behavior.

Signed,

Diana

A Taste of His Own Medicine.

The expression does not mean that the person will literally take medicine.

Perhaps he has been a bully. In the figure above, he's being bullied – getting a "taste of his own medicine."

Chapter 3:
Self-Care and Domestic Living

Hygiene and Grooming

It is very important to maintain good hygiene and grooming. No one wants to be around a person whose hair is messy, whose breath smells bad, whose clothes haven't been washed recently, or who has body odor due to lack of bathing. The letters and replies in this section provide helpful advice about appropriate hygiene and grooming.

Dear Diana,

I'm very close to my friend, Penelope. But recently, she told me that I had developed a body odor and that if I didn't do something about it, she wouldn't be able to go out with me anymore. What should I do?

Signed,

Calliope

Dear Calliope,

In order to avoid smelling bad (body odor), it's important to take a bath or a shower every day. Be sure to use soap and water. Wash your hair often, but not every day. For your hair, use shampoo and conditioner.

Scrub yourself thoroughly, especially under your arms and between your legs. And be sure to put some deodorant under your armpits. (It is called "deodorant" because it helps to de-odor-ize those bad smells.) If you are having your period, use a fresh sanitary pad or tampon after bathing and be sure to change it often. Your bath towels should also be changed often, and your washcloth every day. Once you follow these rules, you'll feel much better about yourself and I know that Penelope will also want to go out with you again.

Signed,

Diana

⌘

Dear Diana,

When I get up in the morning, my mouth feels sticky and I'm worried that my breath smells bad. In fact, the other day, my friend Jorge said to me that my breath did smell bad. He called it "halitosis." I am really upset about this because if Jorge thinks my breath smells bad, it probably does and I can't tell. Please help me.

Signed,

Victor

Dear Victor,

It's hard to tell if your own breath smells bad, but Jorge is probably right. Most people have bad breath when they wake up. Here are a few tips to prevent bad breath.

1. Brush and floss your teeth at least twice a day, after breakfast and before going to bed.
2. If you can't brush your teeth during the day, it's helpful to chew a piece of sugar-free gum for a few minutes after eating.
3. Be sure to change your toothbrush every three months.

4. Visit your dentist every six months. Your dentist might suggest other helpful hints like sucking on sugar-free mints between meals.

I hope these tips help.

Good luck!

Signed,

Diana

⌘

Dear Diana,

I have been told to change my bath towels often and my washcloth every day. But what about my clothes?

Signed,

Hiroko

Dear Hiroko,

Your underwear and socks should be changed every day and always after taking a shower. This is a good idea for shirts and blouses, too. As for pants or skirts and dresses, you need to use your judgment. If they are stained, they should be changed.

Signed,

Diana

⌘

Dear Diana,

I do okay at home, but when I'm out, it's hard to make sure I stay clean and neat. Do you have any advice for me?

Signed,

Mary

Dear Mary,

Yes, I do have some advice. Before you go out, look in the mirror to be sure that your clothes are not stained or torn and that your hair is neat. Always carry a comb and some tissues in your purse or pocket. If you are going out to eat, wash your hands before the meal if you can, but if you can't, carry a small bottle of hand sanitizer or a small package of pre-moistened, sanitized wipes to use before eating. Be prepared by making sure that you always have these items in your purse just in case.

Signed,

Diana

⌘

Here are some more idiomatic expressions.

Dear Diana,

What does the expression "Better late than never" mean?

Signed,

Late Inquirer

Dear Late Inquirer,

The expression means that it's better to do something late than not do it at all. For instance, suppose you received a gift from somebody and didn't write a thank-you note until several weeks later. It's better to have written the thank-you note even though it is late than not to write it at all. Here's another way that the expression is used: If you are driving in snowy conditions, you need to drive slowly and carefully, even if it makes you late. If you drive too fast hoping to be on time, you might get into an accident and never get there at all. So, "better late than never."

Signed,

Diana

⌘

Dear Diana,

What does it mean to "Pay the price"?

Signed,

Price Person

Dear Price Person,

"Paying the price" does not mean that you are actually paying the price for something that you buy. Instead, it refers to the consequences (usually not so pleasant) of doing something that is not generally recommended. For instance, let's say that somebody has a bad habit of smoking cigarettes and develops a cough and lung disease. That person is paying the price for smoking cigarettes.

Signed,

Diana

Dear Diana,

What does the expression "That takes the cake!" mean?

Signed,

Cake Person

Dear Cake Person,

This expression has two meanings. One meaning is "That wins the prize!" (in a contest, for instance). The other meaning is "That does it!" For instance, Carol angrily says, "That takes the cake! I've had it with Maryann insulting my other friends! I don't care to be friends with her any more! She has no business doing that! I'm not putting up with it any more!"

Signed,

Diana

Taking the Cake!

"Taking the cake, literally!"

What "taking the cake really means!" This guy has won all the prizes!

Dear Diana,

One day when I wasn't saying much, my mother asked, "What's the matter, Peggy? Has the cat got your tongue?" I stuck out my tongue to show her that the cat had not got it, but Mom said that was rude. I can see that it was rude, but I was trying to show her that the cat had not got my tongue. So, my question is: What does it mean when somebody asks "Has the cat got your tongue?"

Signed,

Peggy

Dear Peggy,

Your mother was not asking you if the cat had literally removed your tongue. Instead, the expression means "Why aren't you talking?" It could mean that you had nothing to say. It could also mean that you were angry and holding your tongue. This latter expression, "holding your tongue," also means not speaking. Both expressions, although similar, are used differently. When somebody asks you if the cat has got your tongue, he or she wants to know why you aren't talking. If your mother says "hold your tongue," that is a request to stop talking.

Signed,

Diana

Dear Diana,

What does the expression "Fly off the handle" mean?

Signed,

Handle Person

Dear Handle Person,

This expression means losing control of yourself. Let's take an example. John makes a simple suggestion to Peter that one of the shelves in his living room would look less cluttered without so much bric-a-brac on it, recommending putting some of the stuff on another shelf. Even though John is trying to be helpful, Peter gets angry and shouts, "DON'T TELL ME WHAT TO DO! YOU'RE NOT MY AUTHORITY!" With this uncontrolled angry remark, Peter has "flown off the handle."

Signed,

Diana

Dear Diana,

I have been told that the two expressions "Go with the flow" and "Roll with the punches" mean the same thing. But what do they mean?

Signed,

Flow/Punch Inquirer

Dear Flow/Punch Inquirer,

You are absolutely right. These two expressions do mean the same thing. They mean that we have to accept things as they happen in life and not try to change them. If we're swimming in a stream, it's easiest just to float along in the direction the water is taking us. If we're in a boxing match, we have to learn to turn as we are being punched to minimize injury. These expressions also suggest that we need to accept things even if they aren't to our liking. There are stressful things in life that unfortunately we can't control. Trying to fight them gets us nowhere. So, we might as well "go with the flow" and "roll with the punches."

Signed,

Diana

Dear Diana,

What does the expression "By George, I think you've got it!" mean?

Signed,

George

Dear George,

That expression refers to a situation that you are having trouble understanding but suddenly understand.

Signed,

Diana

Dear Diana,

What does the expression "A chip off the old block" mean?

Signed,

Block Chipper

Dear Block Chipper,

If a wood carver is carving something out of wood, soon there will be little chips of the same kind of wood all over the ground. That is the literal meaning of the expression, but we usually use the term to talk about children who are just like their parents. For instance, let's say that the father is reluctant to spend money and the child is reluctant in the same way about eating vegetables. We would say that the child is just like Dad – "a chip off the old block."

Signed,

Diana

Dear Diana,

What does the expression "Call off your dogs" mean?

Signed,

Dog Person

Dear Dog Person,

We say, "Call off your dogs!" to somebody when we want him to stop attacking or criticizing, especially for a minor mistake. For instance, let's say Jane's mom comes downstairs in the morning for breakfast and notices that Jane has cleaned up the kitchen but has left a coffee cup in the sink. Jane's mom goes crazy criticizing her and calling her a slob. Finally, Jane says, "Mom, call off your dogs! It's a just coffee cup."

Signed,

Diana

Dear Diana,

What does the expression "It's a small world" mean?

Signed,

Small One

Dear Small One,

We use that expression when we run into unexpected coincidences. For example, you might find that your neighbors are good friends with your fourth cousins, but you never knew that there was a connection. So, you would say, "Oh, my! It's a small world."

Signed,

Diana

Dear Diana,

What does the expression "On the mend" mean? Does it have anything to do with sewing?

Signed,

Sewing Person

Dear Sewing Person,

If a garment is torn, we "mend" it with a needle and thread. We use a similar expression if somebody is getting better after being sick or hurt.

Signed,

Diana

Dear Diana,

What does the expression "On a roll" mean? Does it have anything to do with a rolling pin?

Signed,

Roll Person

Dear Roll Person,

That means you are experiencing a period of continued success. Therefore, you are on a roll. It has nothing to do with a rolling pin.

Signed,

Diana

Appropriate Dress

It is important to dress properly, but what "proper" means depends on the occasion. For example, you wouldn't wear a tuxedo to a barbecue or a jogging suit to a fancy dinner party. Many companies give employees a uniform to wear while they are working. For example, hospital workers, police officers, and train conductors wear uniforms. Wearing a uniform solves the question of what to wear to work, as long as your uniform is clean and you remember to wear it. If you are performing in a musical event, there is often a dress code. For example, singers may wear white blouses and dark skirts or pants. Church choir members often wear robes. If your work job does not require a uniform, dress in clothing that is not too casual and not stained or torn.

Dear Diana,

I have just received a very fancy invitation to my cousin's wedding. At the bottom of the card, it says "black tie." What does that mean? I don't have any black ties. I only have three neckties and none of them is black.

Signed,

Steve

Dear Steve,

When the invitation says "black tie," it has special meaning. It means that men should wear tuxedos and women should wear fancy evening dresses. It's called "black tie" because a man's tuxedo comes with a black bow tie. If you don't have a tuxedo, you might be able to rent or borrow one or just wear the best dark suit that you own.

Signed,

Diana

⌘

Dear Diana,

Hi, it's Steve again. I bought a tuxedo for my cousin's wedding as you suggested. The wedding was great, but unfortunately, I just learned that my grandmother passed away. Since I just bought it, should I wear my tuxedo to my grandmother's funeral?

Signed,

Steve

Dear Steve,

No, you should not wear a tuxedo to a funeral. This is not an occasion where proper attire is "black tie." Rather, wear a dark, conservative suit and dress shoes; no flip-flops, sneakers, or shorts.

Signed,

Diana

⌘

Dear Diana,

My cousin Mattelle is getting married. She has asked me to be the honorary guest in charge of the guest book. I would be delighted to do that, but I'm not sure exactly how to dress. I have a nice party dress and shoes, but I prefer to wear sneakers since they're much more comfortable. Is that okay?

Signed,

Stacey

Dear Stacey,

No, sneakers are not appropriate for a wedding. I suggest that you wear party shoes and have a good time.

Signed,

Diana

Dear Diana,

What does it mean to "Jump the gun"? Does it have anything to do with real guns? If it does, I'm scared.

Signed,

Scared

Dear Scared,

The expression to "Jump the gun" refers to the starter gun that is used to start a race. If somebody begins the race before the gun goes off, that person is said to have "jumped the gun" and may be disqualified. The expression is also used to mean doing something too soon, especially without thinking carefully about it.

Signed,

Diana

Dear Diana,

My teacher advised me to "Put my best foot forward." Does she mean my left or my right? What exactly does she mean?

Signed,

Janet

Dear Janet,

That expression means to do something as well as you can. It has nothing to do with your left or your right foot. For example, whenever you meet somebody, you always want to put your best foot forward, which means trying to make the best impression you can.

Signed,

Diana

Dear Diana,

What does the expression "Something's fishy around here" mean? Does this have to do with fish?

Signed,

Fish Person

Dear Fish Person,

The expression derives from a term that was originally used when fish were not fresh and began to smell. Now we use the expression to mean that things are not quite right. For example, suppose Michael copied Nelson's math homework. Nelson got problems 3,7, and 11 wrong. When the teacher looks at the papers, she notices that Michael made the exact same three mistakes. So, she says, "Gee, something is fishy around here." This expression is very much like "I smell a rat," which we discussed earlier.

Signed,

Diana

Dear Diana,

What does the expression "Cooking up a storm" mean? I never heard of storms occurring due to cooking.

Signed,

Tom

Dear Tom,

This means that you are cooking an amazing meal. It has nothing to do with bad weather. For example, "Coming home from work today, my mother, who is a good cook, decided that she would cook up a storm tonight. It was a delicious meal."

Signed,

Diana

Health and Nutrition

There are lots of simple things that we can do to help maintain good health, including proper nutrition. Other aspects of healthy living include exercise, understanding the dangers of alcohol and smoking, regular medical check-ups, good eating habits, and a healthy approach to sex.

Dear Diana,

My doctor told me that I have to lose 25 pounds, but she didn't tell me how. She only said that being overweight is not good for my health. What do you think?

Signed,

Jasna

Dear Jasna,

The doctor is right. It's important to maintain a healthy weight. It's not good to be overweight or underweight. Maintaining a healthy weight requires good eating habits, such as eating three meals a day. Don't skip breakfast because if you do, you will be very hungry at lunchtime and may eat too much then.

If you're trying to lose weight, start by cutting down the size of portions you generally eat. Don't take second helpings and don't eat too fast. If you eat fast, you may eat too much before you feel full. Also, use fat-free cream cheese on your toast instead of butter. On salads, try fat-free dressing or none at all. Instead of a rich dessert, try a piece of fruit. Don't eat because you are tired, sad, afraid, angry, depressed, or stressed. (See Chapter 5 on Stress Management.) Only eat when you are hungry.

Signed,

Diana

⌘

Dear Diana,

My Uncle Cecil is on a low-salt diet. He says that's healthy. He also tells me that sugar is not good. What do you think of his advice?

Signed,

Uncle Cecil's Niece

Dear Uncle Cecil's Niece,

I agree with your uncle. Too much salt is not healthy. Go easy on the sugar, too. Most foods don't need extra salt or sugar beyond what is naturally in them. Too much sugar may make you gain weight and is bad for your teeth.

Signed,

Diana

⌘

Dear Diana,

My counselor tells me that it is not a good idea to eat between meals. Why does she say that?

Signed,

Oscar

Dear Oscar,

Your counselor is right. Eating between meals often leads to overeating and weight gain. One way to avoid eating between meals is to brush your teeth after every meal. This is not only good for your teeth, but it leaves your mouth feeling fresh so you will not want to eat again until the next meal.

If you must snack between meals, only have healthy snacks. Never chew gum unless it is sugar-free. Gum with sugar is bad for your teeth.

Signed,

Diana

⌘

Dear Diana,

I live in Macon, Georgia. It gets very hot and humid in the summer. I really hate summers here, but for now I am stuck, stuck, stuck! What advice do you have for dealing with these awful summers in Macon?

Signed,

Benning

Dear Benning,

I'm sure summers in Macon are tough to deal with. Be sure to drink plenty of water so you don't get dehydrated. Use plenty of sunscreen and wear a hat when you go out. Try to avoid going out in sun in the middle of the day. Stay in cool, shady areas. If it's really hot, stay inside with air-conditioning if you have it or at least a fan. This way you will not develop heatstroke – a sickness from being exposed to too much heat.

Signed,

Diana

⌘

Dear Diana,

I just moved from Miami, Florida, to Lake Placid, New York. I have been told that the winters are really cold up here. I hate the cold and want to be sure that I'm ready for it. How do I get ready for winter in Lake Placid? It's November already so I don't have much time before the north winds start to howl!

Signed,

Carlos

Dear Carlos,

You're right. Lake Placid is really cold in the winter. The best advice I can give you is to buy several woolen sweaters. You will also need a warm, woolen hat that covers your ears and a scarf to wear over your face when the wind is blowing. Your pants have to be lined. Thermal underwear can also be very helpful. One little tip: It is best to wear several layers of clothing. If it's bitter cold (and there will be those days!), try not to be outside any longer than necessary. When you come in from being outside, have something hot to drink.

Stay warm.

Signed,

Diana

Exercise

Exercise is important. Find an exercise program that works for you like walking, jogging, or swimming laps. Many people find that it's easier to stick with an exercise program if they have a friend to do it with. If you work out in a fitness center, have somebody show you how to use the equipment properly and safely. It's important to note that almost any exercise program will help you with stress management.

Dear Diana,

I went to the gym for the first time and I think I overdid it, because now the back of both of my legs are sore. Last night, I used a hot water bottle, but I am still sore. What should I do?

Signed,

Achy Agnes

Dear Agnes,

Yes, you are right. You did overdo it. I advise you to stop exercising for just a little while until your legs start feeling normal again. Then you can go back to the gym, starting slowly and only exercising half the time that you did before. Gradually, over several sessions, you can exercise a little bit more until you get to your goal.

Signed,

Diana

Drinking Alcohol

Drinking alcoholic beverages is legal if you are over 21, and many people enjoy them in moderation. But alcohol is tricky, and if you drink too much, it can affect your brain, your judgment, and your health. It is unsafe and against the law to drive when you have been drinking alcoholic beverages. The best way to avoid trouble with alcohol is not to drink it.

Smoking

Smoking is not illegal, but cigarettes are addicting and bad for your health. If you have not started smoking, don't. Besides, in most states, you must be 18 or older to buy cigarettes.

Dear Diana,

I have a bad habit of smoking, which seems to make me cough. I know it's bad for my health to smoke, but I can't seem to stop. I really want to stop smoking. What do you advise me to do?

Signed,

Wayne

Dear Wayne,

It's very hard to stop smoking, but there are professionals who can help you if you are ready to stop. I suggest that you start by asking your doctor to recommend a counselor or a stop-smoking group that can help you.

Good luck!

Signed,

Diana

Sleep

It's important to get enough sleep. If you don't get enough sleep, you'll be tired and grumpy, and you may have difficulty concentrating at school or at work. If you have a complicated task to perform, you can do it much better if you have had enough sleep.

Dear Diana,

At school the other day, my teacher told me that for good nutrition and health, I should eat three square meals a day and that they should be balanced. I have no idea what she was telling me. I am bewildered. Can you explain what she meant?

Signed,

Felix Feeling Flummoxed

Dear Flummoxed Felix,

What the teacher meant by "three square meals" has nothing to do with the shape of the meal but rather what's in it. A square meal is nutritious and contains fruits, vegetables, and sources of protein such as meat, fish, and poultry. If you are a vegetarian, protein options include dairy and soy products. You don't have to eat each of these food sources at every meal, but it is a good idea to try to include them on a daily basis.

Signed,

Diana

Sexual Relationships

People have different attitudes toward sex that often stem from their upbringing, culture, and, of course, personal preferences. Above all, if you are in or are considering a sexual relationship with somebody, be sure to engage in healthy and safe behavior.

Dear Diana,

My boyfriend, Charlie, and I have been close for a very long time. But lately, all he ever seems to have on his mind is sex. This is making me uncomfortable, but I don't want to hurt his feelings. How should I deal with this situation?

Signed,

Maria

Dear Maria,

Sex is not a casual thing. It's not like holding hands, dancing, or hugging and kissing. Sex is the most intimate physical relationship that two people can have, and it should only occur between two people who are strongly attracted to each other and who both want it and understand the consequences.
If you have sex with somebody who is a good friend, it will change the relationship whether you want to or not. In addition, unprotected sex can lead to unplanned pregnancy and sexually

transmitted diseases. It is important for you and Charlie to talk about this. Hopefully, this will avoid any misunderstanding between you.

Stay safe!

Signed,

Diana

⌘

Dear Diana,

I am on birth control pills. I have a new boyfriend and we are getting very intimate. If we have sex, does he need to use a condom?

Signed,

Kathy

Dear Kathy,

Yes! Although birth control pills help to prevent pregnancy, you still need protection from HIV and other sexually transmitted diseases.

Signed,

Diana

⌘

Dear Diana,

John, my boyfriend, sometimes goes around kissing other girls when we are not together, which really hurts my feelings. What should I do?

Signed,

Janet

Dear Janet,

I suggest that you have an open and honest discussion with John, expressing your feelings about his behavior. If he refuses to agree with your strong feelings about the matter, maybe you should break up with him.

Signed,

Diana

Housekeeping and Maintenance

It is important to keep your place neat, orderly, and in good repair. Develop a list of maintenance people whom you can trust. Your list should include a plumber, a painter, an electrician, and a handy person. If you are new to the neighborhood, ask somebody nearby if they have people to recommend. It's always better to get somebody from a personal recommendation than from the Yellow Pages or the Internet.

Dear Diana,

I have to do some spring cleaning, but I don't know how to get started. I have a lot of stuff cluttering up my apartment.

Signed,

Sundeep

Dear Sundeep,

Make a pile of things you wish to keep and another pile of things you wish to get rid of. There may be some items you are not sure about. Make a third pile for them. In a few days, you might have a better idea about what to do with the items in the third pile after you have had a chance to think about it.

Signed,

Diana

Dear Diana,

We have just had a big snowstorm up here in Connecticut and I am snowed in. I'm out of dishwasher detergent. What can I do?

Signed,

James

Dear James,

In a major snowstorm or other emergency, don't go out to buy dishwasher detergent. Dishes can be washed by hand with liquid soap and warm water. Try doing it this way and letting the dishes dry in the dish rack. When the weather gets better, you can go out and shop for dishwasher detergent.

Signed,

Diana

⌘

Dear Diana,

Whenever I do my laundry, my dark clothes always wind up with little white spots of lint on them. What can I do?

Signed,

Olga

Dear Olga,

Separate the darks from the whites. The best way to do this is to have two baskets – one for the darks and another for the whites. After you have separated the clothes, wash them separately. This way you will not get white "pickees" on your clothes.

Signed,

Diana

⌘

Dear Diana,

Yikes! I have discovered that there are roaches in my apartment. What can I do?

Signed,

Lyra

Dear Lyra,

The most important thing is not to have any food where the roaches can get to it. Everything should be in the refrigerator or cupboard and in closed containers. Make sure your pots, pans, cups, dishes, and silverware are clean. Also make sure that the insides of your kitchen drawers are clean and free of food particles. Empty your garbage often and take it outside.

If you still have roaches, go to the hardware store and buy either a spray or a roach trap. Follow the directions for how to use them. If you still have roaches after you have done that, you might have to contact an exterminator. Such companies have special treatments that will get rid of roaches. When the roaches have been exterminated, be sure to follow my instructions so they won't come back.

Signed,

Diana

⌘

Dear Diana,

How can I avoid having to clean up a big mess in my room?

Signed,

Johannes

Dear Johannes,

Big messes usually start with little messes, and occur when we don't put things away after they have been used. To avoid big messes, I suggest that when you're done with one project, put it away before starting something else. This way, you won't have big messes.

Signed,

Diana

⌘

Dear Diana,

I use a mop and a broom to clean my kitchen floor. The rest of my apartment has carpet. What can I do to clean the carpets?

Signed,

Natalie

Dear Natalie,

To clean carpets properly, you need a vacuum cleaner. Vacuum your carpets on a regular basis. It is also a good idea once a year to have a professional cleaning service shampoo your carpets.

Signed,

Diana

⌘

Dear Diana,

What do you recommend to clean furniture that has become dusty?

Signed,

Simone

Dear Simone,

I like to use a spray cleaner for furniture. They have lots of different kinds of spray cleaners at the hardware or grocery store. The best kind of rag to use is an old tee-shirt. I like to call this kind of cleaning "undusting" the furniture.

Signed,

Diana

⌘

Dear Diana,

What do you recommend for cleaning a microwave oven?

Signed,

Betsy

Dear Betsy,

Often warm water and a cloth or paper towel is adequate. However, if there is a major spill or food has stuck to the oven, get a general-purpose kitchen cleaner at the store.

Signed,

Diana

⌘

Dear Diana,

My wife and I have tried getting in contact with Handyman Tom Jones about repairing our broken windowsills. We have left a message on his phone, but he hasn't called back. What can we do?

Signed,

Concerned Homeowner Sam

Dear Sam,

You've got to keep trying. Repair people can be hard to reach. They are probably out doing work for somebody else. Try leaving another message. If he still doesn't call back, call again and ask him to let you know if he has time to do the work or not. Hopefully, that will get his attention. If he still doesn't return your call, you'll have to try somebody else.

Signed,

Diana

⌘

Dear Diana,

I have what looks like a water spot in my ceiling. I first noticed it a few weeks ago, and it is getting bigger. There is a bathroom on the floor above me, but I can't see any place that seems to be leaking. What should I do? Should I call a painter or a plumber?

Signed,

Marcia

Dear Marcia,

Call a licensed plumber to look at this problem. There's no point in calling a painter now. First, you have to find the source of the leak and have it repaired. As long as the plumber is coming, check around to see if you have any other problems, such as leaky faucets, running toilets, or clogged drains. That way you'll only have to wait for the plumber once and he can do all the repairs in one day. After the plumber has fixed the leak, wait a few days to be sure that the leak has really been fixed. Then, call the painter.

Signed,

Diana

⌘

Dear Diana,

I'm having a problem. Every time I turn on the water in my kitchen sink, it leaks. I called the plumber, but the only day he can come this week is Friday and I have to work on Friday.

Signed,

Owner of Leaky Sink

Dear Owner of Leaky Sink,

Stop using the sink until it has been fixed. I think that you should call your boss to explain the situation and ask for the day off so that you can get this problem attended to before you have a big flood. Alternatively, you could call another plumber who might be more readily available.

Signed,

Diana

Cooking

Eating out with friends is great, but if you eat out too often, it can become expensive. In general, home cooked food is much healthier than restaurant food. Besides, if you are eating at home, you have much better control over the portion sizes.

Dear Diana,

When I lived at home, my mom did all the cooking and I didn't pay any attention to what she did. Now I'm on my own and want to learn how to cook. How do I get started?

Signed,

Armen

Dear Armen,

There are plenty of cookbooks and cooking websites with simple recipes. I recommend finding recipes with lots of illustrations. Always wash your hands thoroughly with soap and water before beginning to cook to prevent the spread of germs. Read through a recipe and assemble all the ingredients and cookware before starting to cook in case you need to defrost something or go back to the store for an ingredient. Maybe you should consider a cooking class for beginners, if there is one in your neighborhood.

Signed,

Diana

⌘

Dear Diana,

I was cooking spaghetti the other day when the phone rang. I answered the phone and while my back was turned, the water boiled over and spilled onto the cooktop and the floor. What should I have done with the phone ringing and the water boiling?

Signed,

Luigi

Dear Luigi,

Never leave something that is cooking on the stove unattended, even for a moment. If you must answer the phone or doorbell or leave the kitchen for any reason, turn the burner off until you come back.

Signed,

Diana

⌘

Dear Diana,

I live alone and usually cook for myself. But it's a bother cooking a whole meal for one person. What do you do?

Signed,

Rachel the Cook

Dear Rachel,

When I cook for myself, I often cook enough for several meals. For example, I love chicken. In the grocery store, chicken parts usually come in packages, and there is too much meat in a package for one person. The best thing to do is to cook all the chicken at once and then divide the cooked chicken into portions. Keep one portion in the refrigerator to eat that night. For the remaining portions, wrap individual meal portions of the chicken separately in plastic wrap or a baggie and put them in the freezer. In this way, you can take one portion out at a time. If you are having a lot of people over for dinner, don't put anything in the freezer until after the party. Then, if there are leftovers, make portions, again meal-size, and freeze them separately, as I have described. This method works for practically anything you want to cook, like macaroni, lasagna, mashed potatoes, string beans, etc.

Signed,

Diana

⌘

Dear Diana,

I have just come home from work. I'm tired and hungry. I don't feel like cooking and I want to cut back on eating out. What should I do?

Signed,

Tired and Hungry

Dear Tired and Hungry,

I just wrote to Rachel the Cook and gave her advice about this very situation. If you had frozen away meal-sized portions from a previous day, you could have taken a portion out of the freezer, defrosted and warmed it in the microwave oven. If you have a can of soup (I always have several cans of soup in the cupboard), you could open it, pour the soup in a microwave-proof bowl, and heat it up. If you have cold-cuts in the refrigerator, you could make a sandwich. A peanut butter and jelly sandwich can also be made very quickly.

Signed,

Diana

⌘

Expressions, expressions,
They are so much fun.
So I have some more,
And soon I'll be done.

Dear Diana,

What does the expression "You've gone too far!" mean?

Signed,

Gone too Far

Dear Gone too Far,

To "go too far" means to do more than is acceptable. For example, when Becky visited her friend Catherine, she helped clean up Catherine's bedroom. However, Becky not only cleaned up the bedroom, she also put away the clothing that Catherine had picked out and laid on a chair to be worn the next day. Becky went too far.

Signed,

Diana

Dear Diana,

When I got my job supervisor's permission to take time off to visit my parents, he said, "Be my guest," but how can I be his guest? He has never invited me to his place for dinner to be his guest. I'm confused.

Signed,

John

Dear John,

What your supervisor meant when he told you "Be my guest" was that "You have my permission to take that time off to visit your parents." This is a common expression. It means "That's just fine, whatever you want to do," because that's the way you would treat a guest.

Signed,

Diana

Dear Diana,

When I told my friend Lauren that somebody had sneaked into my pocketbook and stolen my money, she told me, "Well, join the club!" I am so confused. I have no idea what club she is talking about.

Signed,

Melissa

Dear Melissa,

That expression indicates that your friend has been in the same or a similar unfortunate state as you. That is, Lauren meant that her money had been stolen, too. It has nothing to do with joining a club.

Signed,

Diana

Dear Diana,

We offered my Aunty Susan some banana bread. She said, "No, thank you." Then she added, "It's not my cup of tea." Well, of course, it isn't; it's banana bread! Why did she add that line?

Signed,

Julie

Dear Julie,

Aunty Susan is using an expression to indicate that she doesn't care for banana bread. This is a polite expression for saying, "Julie, I don't like banana bread."

Signed,

Diana

Dear Diana,

We just hired a new cleaning lady, Martha. On her very first day of work, she was so rude that my mother fired her. My father said that Martha "Got off on the wrong foot." What has her foot got to do with it?

Signed,

Megan

Dear Megan,

Your father simply meant that Martha had started her job as a new cleaning lady badly. "To get off on the wrong foot" means that something isn't working from the outset.

Signed,

Diana

(If you are reading carefully, you will realize that Martha did not "put her best foot forward." See page 91.)

Dear Diana,

I broke my mother's favorite vase by accident, but I lied and told her that I hadn't done it. After my mom found out that it was me after all, she said I was "Pulling the wool over her eyes." What did she mean by that expression?

Signed,

Katie

Dear Katie,

If you're trying to "Pull the wool over somebody's eyes," it means you're trying to deceive to prevent them from knowing what you are really doing. When your mother said that you were pulling the wool over her eyes, it meant that she knew what you were up to – trying to deceive her.

Signed,

Diana

Chapter 4:
Getting Around, Employment, and Community Participation

Public Transportation

Many people with special needs don't drive cars and, therefore, depend upon public transportation. For short distances, the best way to get around is to take buses, the subway (metro), or taxicabs. For longer distances, the best way is to go by plane or train. In this chapter, I offer some helpful tips that will ensure that your trips are safe and pleasant.

Accessing and Reading a Bus Schedule

Schedules can be confusing but if you follow the suggestions below, you'll soon get the hang of it.

Dear Diana,

I just got a new job in downtown New Haven, Connecticut, too far away for me to walk to. I think I can get there by bus but don't know which bus to take, when the buses go, and where the bus stops are. Can you help me?

Signed,

Megan

Dear Megan,

The first thing you need is a bus schedule. There are several ways to get one. Let's say that you want to go from Chapel Haven, which is located at 1040 Whalley Avenue in New Haven, to The New Haven Green, which is in the middle of town. You could call Connecticut Transit (CTTransit) and ask them. The number to call for the bus schedules is usually posted at the bus stop. If you call, you have to write the schedule down. Therefore, you'll need to have a pencil and paper handy. Some bus stops, especially the busy ones, have the schedules posted on a signpost right there. If you have access to the Internet, you can also find schedules there and then print it out.

Signed,

Diana

⌘

Dear Diana,

I followed your advice and printed out the bus schedule from the website of CTTransit. But I'm having trouble reading it. It is very confusing to me. Can you give me any tips on how to read a bus schedule?

Signed,

Megan

Dear Megan,

I agree. Reading a bus schedule can be confusing. An example of a bus schedule is shown on page 119. You will find Westville on the bus schedule. The bus schedule lists what time the bus leaves Westville and what time it arrives in downtown New Haven. For example, a bus, called the B bus, leaves Westville

Center at 8:20 AM and arrives at downtown New Haven at 8:37 AM. You will notice that it makes a stop before New Haven at Whalley and Boulevard at 8:25 AM.

To decide which bus to take, you need to know when you must be at work. Don't cut it too close or you will be late for work. It is best to arrive early, so that you have plenty of time to get from the bus stop to your job. Let's say it takes 5 minutes to walk from the bus stop to your workplace. The B bus that leaves at 8:20 from Westville is your best choice because it allows enough time to walk from the downtown New Haven Stop to your workplace.

Good luck on your first day of work!

Signed,

Diana

PS. You might want to practice the bus route you are going to take *before* your first day on the job. This way, you will be sure not to be late.

Bus Schedule and Copy of a Bus Route.

Timepoints	7	6	4	5	3	2	8	
Route	Brookside Terminus Augustine Street	Southern CT State University Fitch Street	Jewish Community Center	Amity Road Terminus Amity Shopping Center	Westville Center Whalley & Blake	Whalley & Boulevard	Downtown New Haven Temple & Chapel	Continues to route
B7	4:56	5:02	..	..	5:06	5:09	5:20	B7
BO	..	..	..	5:32	5:41	5:44	5:55	BO
B6	5:46	5:52	..	..	5:56	5:59	6:10	B6
B4	..	..	..	6:02	6:11	6:14	6:25	B4
B6	6:13	6:19	..	..	6:23	6:26	6:37	B6
B4	..	..	..	6:29	6:38	6:41	6:52	B4
B7	6:34	6:41	..	..	6:45	6:50	7:02	B7
B4	..	..	..	6:46	6:55	7:00	7:12	B4
B6	6:54	7:01	..	..	7:05	7:10	7:22	B6
B	..	..	..	7:01	7:10	7:15	7:27	..
B4	7:09	7:16	..	..	7:20	7:25	7:37	B4
B7	..	..	..	7:21	7:30	7:35	7:47	B7
B	7:29	7:36	..	..	7:40	7:45	7:57	B
B4	..	..	7:31	7:41	7:50	7:55	8:07	B4
B5	7:49	7:56	..	..	8:00	8:05	8:17	B5
B4	7:59	8:06	..	..	8:10	8:15	8:27	B4
B	..	..	..	8:11	8:20	8:25	Y8:37	B
B4	8:19	8:26	..	..	8:30	8:35	8:47	B4
B7	8:29	8:36	..	..	8:40	8:45	8:57	B7
B4	..	..	8:31	8:45	8:54	8:59	9:12	B4
B	8:49	8:57	..	..	9:02	9:07	9:20	..
B5	9:01	9:09	..	..	9:14	9:19	9:32	B5
B4	..	..	9:11	9:20	9:29	9:34	9:47	B4
B7	9:31	9:39	..	..	9:44	9:49	10:02	B7
B4	..	..	..	9:50	9:59	10:04	10:17	B4
B5	10:01	10:09	..	..	10:14	10:19	10:32	B5
B4	..	..	10:11	10:20	10:29	10:34	10:47	B4
B7	10:31	10:39	..	..	10:44	10:49	11:02	B7
B4	..	..	..	10:50	10:59	11:04	11:17	B4
B5	11:01	11:09	..	..	11:14	11:19	11:32	B5

The routing and times of a typical bus schedule are shown here. Above are the numbers of the buses and the times that they will arrive at their stops.

Proper Behavior on the Bus

When boarding the bus, you are expected to pay by dropping the proper fare in the fare box. Most fare boxes require exact change, so be sure that you know how much the fare is and have the exact change ready. If you have a special bus pass, you must show it to the bus driver. If you need to transfer to another bus, ask the bus driver for a transfer slip. There is no extra charge for the transfer slip.

Dear Diana,

I need advice about how to behave on the bus when the bus is in motion and after the bus has stopped. Can you help me?

Signed,

New Bus Rider

Dear New Bus Rider,

Here are my ABCs for proper bus behavior.

1. On the bus, avoid contact with strangers. To help you avoid getting into conversations with strangers, bring something to read or music to listen to (use earphones).
2. Use the handrails if you must stand up when there are no seats available.
3. Don't stand in the step well at the back of the bus. DOORS MAY OPEN UNEXPECTEDLY!
4. Keep your head, arms, and legs inside the bus at all times. This is particularly true in the summer when it is hot and the bus windows might be open.
5. Don't engage in cell phone conversations on the bus. If you must use your cell phone for an urgent call, keep your voice low and make the call short.

6. Don't bother others on the bus. Especially, don't talk to the bus driver while the bus is in motion. You can talk to your friends on the bus as long as you are considerate of others.
7. Do not eat, drink, or smoke on the bus.
8. Keep the aisles clear of your things.
9. If you have nothing to read on the bus, sit back, relax, and enjoy your ride. Sit quietly in your seat and look out the window at all the scenery.

Good luck with my ABCs of proper bus behavior.

Signed,

Diana

⌘

Dear Diana,

In the very back of the bus where I usually sit, this strange guy makes fun of me just because I am wearing glasses for reading. He calls me "four eyes!" I don't like it and it hurts my feelings. What can I do?

Signed,

Eyeglass Wearer

Dear Eyeglass Wearer,

If you ever are bothered on the bus for any reason, move to the front of the bus, close to the driver. That way people are less likely to bother you. If necessary, inform the driver if somebody is bothering you.

Signed,

Diana

⌘

Dear Diana,

What do I do when there are no seats available on the bus?

Signed,

Seatless Rider

Dear Seatless Rider,

If you have a physical disability, there are seats at the front of the bus reserved for the handicapped and for senior citizens. If you don't have a physical disability, you will have to stand up until a seat becomes available. This should not be a problem as long as you're young and healthy. Always use the hand rails while standing. Good luck!

Signed,

Diana

⌘

Dear Diana,

I need some advice about how to notify the bus driver that I want to get off at the next stop. I know that it's rude to shout to the bus driver and improper to walk up to the front of the bus to distract the driver. What should I do?

Signed,

Rider Who Wants to Deboard

Dear Rider,

All buses have a "STOP REQUEST" bell that you sound by pulling a chain or touching a yellow tape. This bell notifies the bus driver that a passenger wants to get off at the next stop. Next time you are on the bus, look for that bell and be prepared to pull the chain or touch the tape when you want to get off at the next stop. You will know that you have done it right when you see the sign light up in front of the bus that says “STOP REQUESTED.”

Signed,

Diana

Taxis

Taxis are convenient because you don’t have to follow a schedule or walk to the bus stop or train station and wait. But in the long run, it can become expensive, so taking cabs is usually not a good choice for everyday transportation.

Dear Diana,

I missed my bus again! My boss said that if I’m late one more time, I’ll lose my job. I don’t want to lose my job, no way! Maybe when I find myself short of time, I should take a taxi. How do I do that?

Signed,

Tardy Tom

Dear Tardy Tom,

Taxicabs can be convenient, because they are usually faster than buses and they take you directly to your destination. When you have a lot of groceries, taxicabs are often the best choice. When you don’t have enough time to take the bus, taking a taxicab may be necessary. However, taking cabs costs much more than buses. The amount you have to pay will depend upon how many miles you have to travel.

You can either board the cab at a taxi stand, hail one, or phone for one. If you phone for one, be sure to tell them exactly where you are, where you would like to go, and how many passengers there will be. Ask how many minutes before the taxicab will be arriving and how much the fare will be. For advice about tipping the taxi driver, see the section on life skills on page 11.

Signed,

Diana

Accessing and Reading a Train Schedule

Train travel can be convenient if you live in parts of the country where commuter trains are common, like the Northeast. Amtrak is a train service that is widely available. Blondie has just written a letter to me about Amtrak. Let's use her letter as an example.

Dear Diana,

I live in Boston, and want to visit my parents in Providence. It seems like the train would be more convenient for me than the bus. I have never traveled on Amtrak before, but I've been told that there is good service between Boston and Providence. How do I find out more information?

Signed,

Blondie

Dear Blondie,

You are right: Amtrak can be a great way to travel from Boston to Providence or between many other cities that have Amtrak service. You need to get an Amtrak schedule. One way to do this is to call 1-800-USA-RAIL (1-800-872-7245), which is the toll-free Amtrak telephone number that works anywhere in the United States. Other train systems, like MetroNorth for the Greater New York region, have their own telephone numbers.

When you call Amtrak, you will get an automated reply. Be prepared to answer the questions that the automated voice asks. If you get confused or if the automated voice cannot understand you, you will be asked to repeat what you said. If the automated voice still can't understand your reply, say as clearly as possibly, "agent." You will then be connected to a live person. Speaking to the live Amtrak agent, you can ask your questions directly.

This should work for you, Blondie.

Signed,

Diana

⌘

Dear Diana,

Hi! It's Blondie again. I have another question about train schedules. Can I get them on the Internet?

Signed,

Your Train Pal, Blondie

Dear Blondie,

Yes you can! Simply log on to the website of the train system, such as Amtrak.com. When you log on, you will see a box that says SCHEDULES. Click on that box. You will be directed to fill in the date, time, and place you are starting from and going to. After you fill in the information, you get a bar that says "See Schedules." Click on that bar, and the schedule will appear with several choices. See the sample below. Choose the time when you want to leave.

Signed,

Diana

Amtrak Schedule From Boston, MA, to Providence, RI.

Schedules

Monday, December 30, 2013
From: Boston, MA - Back Bay (BBY)
To: Providence, RI (PVD)

Depart	Arrive	Connection	Duration*	Route	Train (Bus) #
Mon 5:15 am	Mon 5:45 am	Direct	0 hr, 30 min	Acela Express	2151
Mon 6:15 am	Mon 6:50 am	Direct	0 hr, 35 min	Northeast Regional	95
Mon 7:20 am	Mon 7:50 am	Direct	0 hr, 30 min	Acela Express	2155
Mon 8:20 am	Mon 8:54 am	Direct	0 hr, 34 min	Northeast Regional	171
Mon 9:20 am	Mon 9:50 am	Direct	0 hr, 30 min	Acela Express	2159
Mon 9:41 am	Mon 10:13 am	Direct	0 hr, 32 min	Northeast Regional	93
Mon 11:11 am	Mon 11:44 am	Direct	0 hr, 33 min	Northeast Regional	173
Mon 11:20 am	Mon 11:51 am	Direct	0 hr, 31 min	Acela Express	2163
Mon 12:20 pm	Mon 12:48 pm	Direct	0 hr, 28 min	Acela Express	2165
Mon 1:21 pm	Mon 1:51 pm	Direct	0 hr, 30 min	Acela Express	2167

*Total duration does not include time between connecting services.

Dear Diana,

Sorry to be such a pest, but it's Blondie again! I followed your instructions and know what train I want to take from Boston to Providence. I don't have a credit or debit card but have cash to purchase my train ticket. What do I do next?

Signed,

Blondie, Again

Dear Blondie, Again,

You're not a pest! You need to purchase your train ticket ahead of time at the station. Print out the travel information from the Internet so that you will have it with you. Go to the ticket window at the train station and tell the ticket agent what train you want to take. Make sure you know how much the ticket will cost beforehand and bring enough cash.

If you are traveling on a very busy holiday weekend, purchase your ticket at least two weeks in advance. Be sure to get your return ticket at the same time. Once you've purchased your tickets, be sure to keep them in a safe place. Blondie, have a great trip to Providence!

Signed,

Diana

⌘

Dear Diana,

I have followed the very good advice that you have given to Blondie, and I am all set. But I'm not sure what to do when I get to the train station. Can you help Blondie and me a bit more?

Signed,

Lonnie

Dear Lonnie,

On the day of your trip, arrive at the train station at least 30 minutes before your train is scheduled to depart. Be sure to know your train number. It's printed on your ticket. There is an information board at the train station telling you if the train is on time and what track it is leaving from. They do not usually give the track number until shortly before the train arrives at the station, so you've got to keep an eye on the board. Once the track number is announced, go to the track right away. When the train comes in, the conductor will announce the train number and where the train is going. If there is any doubt in your mind, show the conductor your ticket and ask if it's the right train. If you are not sure when to get off the train, listen for the announcement. You can also ask the conductor to remind you when the train is arriving at your stop. Always be polite to the conductors. They are there to help you. It's okay to ask for help if you need it.

Have a great trip!

Signed,

Diana

Traveling by Plane

Especially when traveling long distances and to parts of the country where train and bus service is poor or nonexistent, taking a plane is often the best solution. Some of the general recommendations about finding schedules and how to behave on board are the same for all kinds of public transportation, but flying poses many unique challenges these days.

Dear Diana,

I live in North Carolina and would like to visit my friend in California. According to the schedules, going by bus or train would take several days, so maybe I will go by plane. I have never taken a plane before. Do you have any advice about taking a plane across the country?

Signed,

Samantha

Dear Samantha,

For plane trips, I advise that you get assistance from your counselors, family members, or a travel agent. Plane tickets always have to be purchased in advance and can be expensive. Your ticket or reservation will show your flight number, so that you can confirm your flight on-line or by phone. You need to know what terminal and gate your plane is departing from. This is sometimes on your boarding pass but sometimes not. You have to look at the monitors at the airport to check or recheck the boarding gate and the time of departure. Like the train, the time of departure of the plane may be delayed. The gate that the plane is leaving from is also subject to change. Passengers are generally advised to get to the airport at least an hour before the plane is scheduled to leave, but it is better to give yourself more time, like two hours, so that you won't cut it too close.

Signed,

Diana

⌘

Dear Diana,

It sounds like flying to California won't be so easy. I've heard about all kinds of hassles at the airport. Can you tell me about that?

Signed,

Samantha

Dear Samantha,

The biggest hassle is getting through what they call Security. You have to have a picture ID and also a boarding pass before you are allowed to enter the security line. There are many rules about what you can and cannot carry onto the airplane. In order to get through the security check, you have to take off your shoes, coat, and jacket, if you are wearing one. You also have to place whatever is in your pocket (keys, wallet, etc.) in a small plastic bowl or rubber tray. It goes through the security conveyor belt separately, and you get everything back after you go through the screening machine yourself. With some of the modern scanners, called body scanners, you can't even have a handkerchief or tissue in your pocket! If you have a computer, it has to be taken out, placed on the rubber tray, and sent through separately. You will get your computer back also, after you go through the scanning machine. Knives and any sharp objects are not allowed at any time. If you happen to have one, the security agent will take it away from you and not give it back. Some airports won't even allow knitting needles. You cannot take any more than three ounces of water (less than half a glass!). It is a real bother! If you have a water bottle, it will have to be emptied before you are allowed to take it with you. Once you have passed the security check, you can refill your water bottle (if you can find a drinking fountain) or buy a bottle of water or soda to take on the plane.

Also, no jokes are allowed when you are going through Security. For example, you would never say, "I have something in my pocket, ha ha!!!" If you do, the security guards will pull you aside and ask all kinds of questions which may get you into big trouble and also make you miss your plane!

So, the short message about traveling by air is that you need time to spare. On the other hand, it is the only convenient way to travel across the country.

Signed,

Diana

Employment and Workplace Behavior

Getting a job is a major, often difficult, step, but it doesn't end there. The workplace comes with its own set of rules for proper behavior that are important to follow in order to keep a job.

Getting a Job

When deciding it's time to get a job, it is important to first think of job that you would like and that fits your personality and skills. Once that's in place, the next step is to start looking for such a position by asking friends, family, counselors, etc., as well as checking online, in the daily newspaper, and postings in stores.

Dear Diana,

I would like to have a job for two reasons. First, I need money for my needs and wants. Second, without a job, I have too much time on my hands and get bored. I'm not sure how to find a job. Can you help me?

Signed,

Jobless Joe

Dear Joe,

There are jobs in grocery stores, offices, department stores, restaurants, pharmacies, beauty parlors, car washes, banks, post offices, art and frame shops, hotels – all kinds of jobs. Some positions might involve cleaning, others stocking things on shelves or stuffing envelopes. Some are in a dry cleaning business. What kind of job would you like to have? What do you enjoy and what are you good at?

Signed,

Diana

⌘

Dear Diana,

I love to clean. When I clean a place, any place, it makes me feel good. Do you think I could get a job where I would get paid to clean?

Signed,

Jobless Joe,

Dear Joe,

Yes, absolutely. Here are a few steps to consider. You can ask your vocational counselor to help you. If you don't have a vocational counselor, you can look in the Help Wanted section of a current issue of your local newspaper. Your friends or relatives might also know about a job for you. Sometimes, stores post a "Help Wanted" ad in the window. If so, you can go inside and ask what kind of a job they have available.

The next step is to apply for the job. In order to do that, you usually need to complete an application form, which consists of filling out information about you, such as your name, address, phone number, e-mail, and social security number. The application also asks about your background, such as whether you graduated from high school and when. If you went to college, you also record that information where requested. The rest of the application generally consists of answering questions related to why you are applying for the job. In this section, you will need to explain why you think you are appropriate for the job. If the application is difficult for you to fill out by yourself, ask your vocational counselor to help you. If you don't have a vocational counselor, perhaps a family member or friend can help you.

I'm sure that you will find a good job.

Signed,

Diana

⌘

Dear Diana,

Hooray! I got a job! I am so happy but also nervous. What if I don't do the job right and get fired?

Signed,

Joe With a Job!

Dear Joe,

Congratulations on getting a job! I'm so happy for you. Now comes the big challenge: doing your work well and keeping the job. Once you have been hired, it's important to show your boss that they picked the right person. To do that, you must come to work on time, well groomed, well rested, and ready to work. On your first day, your boss or supervisor will explain to you what you are expected to do. It's important to pay close attention to these instructions. Sometimes, it is not easy to understand all aspects of the job. If you have any questions, be sure to ask so you understand what you are expected to do.

Some programs provide a job coach to help you get started. For the first few days, the job coach will go with you to make sure that you do your job properly. Once you understand the job and are able to perform it independently, you no longer need a job coach on a regular basis. From then on, the job coach will come every once in a while to make sure that you are still doing your job properly.

Again, congratulations. I am sure that you will do well!

Signed,

Diana

Workplace Behavior

Goofing off, joking around, and similar behaviors that you might engage in with your friends on your own time are usually not appropriate in the workplace. Below are some particularly important things to remember when you are at work.

Dear Diana,

I got a job a year ago. Everything was fine for a while, but now I'm having trouble. My boss is constantly reminding me to pay attention to my work and not get into long conversations with coworkers unrelated to my job. Besides, I had an issue with one of my coworkers and we were both called into the boss's office. I am worried that I'll lose my job. What should I do?

Signed,

Worried Willie

Dear Willie,

If you are having problems with your coworkers, it's a good idea to talk to your boss or your vocational counselor before the problem gets out of hand. From your letter, it sounds like something you need to do. I don't know if your boss is also concerned about your attitude. Don't forget that it is important to maintain a positive attitude on the job. Companies don't keep employees with poor attitudes. Here are a few more things to remember.

1. Follow the rules of the job. For example, when it is work time, you should be working. When you are on your lunch break, you are expected to eat your lunch. It is not appropriate to eat your lunch when you are supposed to be

working. 2. Work until your work is finished. If you finish early, ask your boss what else there is to do. 3. Never leave your job to go home until your work hours are finished unless you have been given permission. 4. Remember that your work is being evaluated like getting a report card in school. So, you should always do your very best.

Signed,

Diana

Dear Diana,

What do I do if my mobile phone rings while I'm at work?

Signed,

Joan

Dear Joan,

Turn off your phone when you get to work. That way, you won't hear it ringing and you won't be tempted to answer it. You can get messages later, for example, during breaks, lunch, or after work.

Signed,

Diana

⌘

Dear Diana,

Part of my job is to clean up the break room, but I'm not sure what to do if a lot of people are on break or having lunch.

Signed,

Mike

Dear Mike,

Do your best to clean up without bothering coworkers. Also, it may be a good idea to ask your supervisor for suggestions.

Signed,

Diana

⌘

Dear Diana,

I cannot go to work next Monday because I have a doctor's appointment. What should I do?

Signed,

Carol

Dear Carol,

Get permission from your supervisor ahead of time. If you have to miss work because of an emergency, call your supervisor that morning, but don't let this happen too often.

Signed,

Diana

For more expressions,
It is time.
Do enjoy
My special rhyme.

Dear Diana,

My parents told me that I'm on the "Crest of a wave" because I'm doing so well with lots of things. That's great, but what can a crest and a wave possibly have to do with my doing well?

Signed,

Steve

Dear Steve,

The best ride on a surfboard is on the crest of a wave. That's where the expression comes from. The term is usually used to mean that you are performing at your very best. It may also mean that you are on a roll. (See earlier discussion of that idiom "on a roll" on page 88.)

Signed,

Diana

Dear Diana,

My Uncle Paul's favorite baseball team is the Boston Red Sox. They lost last year. He is convinced that this year they will win, but Aunty Jill says he's just "Whistling in the dark." I haven't noticed that and wonder what whistling in the dark has to do with the Boston Red Sox.

Signed,

Stacey

Dear Stacey,

When Aunty Jill used that expression "Whistling in the dark," she meant that Uncle Paul was just wishing and hoping that the Red Sox would win without any reason for thinking that they would.

Signed,

Diana

Dear Diana,

My math teacher tells me that if I "Can't cut the mustard" in the class, I won't learn anything. What does mustard have to do with succeeding in class?

Signed,

Lisa

Dear Lisa,

This is a silly expression because you cannot really cut mustard. When we use this expression we mean we can't deal with challenges successfully. What the teacher meant then was "If you don't master the subject matter in the math class, you will not meet the challenge."

Signed,

Diana

Dear Diana,

What does the expression "Don't throw the baby out with the bath water" mean?

Signed, Confused About Bath water

Dear Confused,

Here's an example: Suppose you are writing a book or a document and you have repeated the same information too many times. You need to delete some of it, but you don't want to delete the entire book. In the same way, after you give a baby a bath, you throw out the bath water, but definitely not the baby! Here's another example: You found some outdated mayonnaise in your refrigerator. As a result, you decided to go through the refrigerator looking for other outdated items, but you probably don't need to throw out everything. That would be like "throwing the baby out with the bath water."

Signed,

Diana

Throwing out the Baby With the Bath Water.

The expression doesn't mean that a baby is actually thrown out of the bath with the bath water, as shown above.

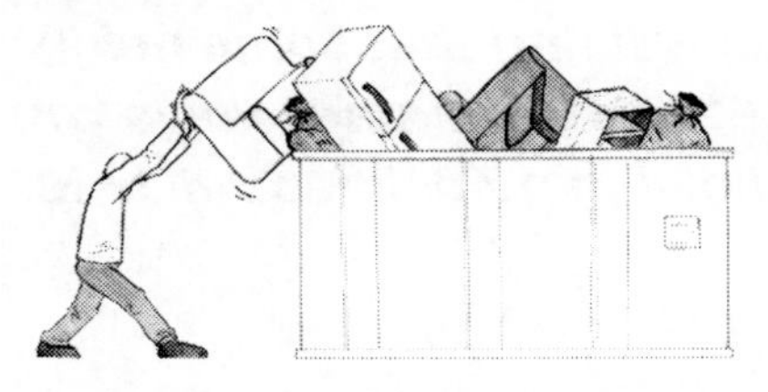

What the expression really means is that instead of getting rid of one household item, for example, you wind up getting rid of everything in your house, as shown above.

Dear Diana,

What does the expression "Down in the dumps" mean?

Signed,

Dumps Inquirer

Dear Dumps Inquirer,

The expression means being miserable, sad, blue, grumpy, depressed, grouchy, or experiencing other negative feelings. It does not mean that you have gone into the garbage dump. For example, you are counting on going to the movies with your friend, but she calls to tell you that she can't make it because she is going out with another friend. You are not happy about this and feel disappointed. Therefore, you are feeling "down in the dumps."

Signed,

Diana

Neighbors

Always do your best to be cordial, and before you know it, you will find that some neighbors can also be friends and that there are many ways you can help each other. The following guidelines will help.

Dear Diana,

I'm worried that some day I will forget my house keys and end up being locked out of my apartment. What can I do to prevent this from happening?

Signed,

Paul

Dear Paul,

If you have neighbors whom you have known for a while and can trust, consider asking them to keep an extra set of your keys in their place. This way, if you forget your keys, you can go over to your neighbors, pick up your keys, and let yourself in. Don't forget to give the extra set of house keys back to your neighbors afterwards in case you lock yourself out again. You might also consider leaving a set of spare house keys in a hidden location on your property that nobody else will be able to find.

Signed,

Diana

⌘

Dear Diana,

I'm going out of town for about a week and need to make arrangements for my plants to be watered and my mail to be picked up. What do you advise?

Signed,

Katherine

Dear Katherine,

As I advised Paul, my best suggestion is to choose a neighbor you know and trust and ask him or her to do these favors for you. In return, offer to do the same for your neighbors when they go away.

Signed,

Diana

Community Awareness

Living independently in a community requires you to be aware of both routine and emergency services. For example, you will want to know about community activities, which you can do by reading the local newspaper, checking websites, and talking to people. You will also want to know where the essential stores are, such as the pharmacy, grocery store, bank, the post office, the dry cleaners, bus stops, etc. It is also important to know how to contact emergency services. I suggest posting a list of emergency telephone numbers with a magnet on your refrigerator. The list should include telephone numbers for the police, fire department, ambulance, and poison control center.

Dear Diana,

Help! I have just moved into a new neighborhood. I need a grocery store, a dry cleaners, a pharmacy, and a bank. I also need to find out where the post office and the library are. Finally, I need to find some maintenance people because my new place needs painting and some other work. Where should I turn?

Signed,

Guillermo

Dear Guillermo,

If you used a real estate agent to find your new place, he or she may know how to find these services. In addition, this is a good reason to introduce yourself to your neighbors. Once you've done that, you can ask them where they shop and obtain services. The local newspaper often has ads for local businesses, but it is better to get a personal reference from a neighbor, especially for someone who is going to work in your home.

Good luck with your new home!

Signed,

Diana

It's time for more expressions.

Dear Diana,

What does the expression "It serves you right" mean?

Signed,

Served Right Inquirer

Dear Served Right Inquirer,

The expression means "You get what you deserve!" It is usually used when somebody has behaved badly or carelessly and is now paying for it. Let's say you complain, "Mary never calls me," and your mother says, "Well, it serves you right. You weren't very nice to her. So, now you've lost her friendship."

Signed,

Diana

Dear Diana,

What does the expression "Look at the bright side" mean?

Signed,

Bright Side

Dear Bright Side,

Okay, let's say that your friend called you saying that she had to cancel your date because something had suddenly come up. You're disappointed, but you're now free to visit your grandparents – a trip you would otherwise have missed. So the cancelled date with your friend makes you sad, but the bright side is that you get to visit your grandparents.

Signed,

Diana

Dear Diana,

What does the expression "If you can't beat them, join them" mean?

Signed,

Beat/Join Person

Dear Beat/Join Person,

I hope the following explains this commonly used term. Mary and Joe decided to stop cutting their grass because they wanted to make their backyard look like a meadow. But after a few weeks, the neighbors started to complain because everybody else's lawns were neatly mowed. Mary and Joe decided it wasn't worth the hassle and mowed their lawn, agreeing, "If you can't beat them, join them."

Signed,

Diana

Dear Diana,

What does the expression "You're getting the hang of it" mean? Does it have anything to do with a clothesline?

Signed,

Puzzled

Dear Puzzled,

"Getting the hang of it" means that you're learning how to do something very well on your own. It has nothing to do with a clothesline.

Signed,

Diana

Dear Diana,

What does the expression "It's raining cats and dogs" mean?

Signed,

Cat and Dog Inquirer

Dear Cat and Dog Inquirer,

It means that it's really raining hard – and has nothing literally to do with cats and dogs.

Signed,

Diana

Raining Cats and Dogs!

In the figure above, you can see cats and dogs are coming down with the rain. This never happens!

What the expression really means is that it's raining very, very hard, as shown above.

Dear Diana,

What does the expression "Sticks and stones may break my bones, but words will never hurt me" mean?

Signed,

Stick and Stone Inquirer

Dear Stick and Stone Inquirer,

Sticks and stones cause physical injuries, but words only hurt emotionally and psychologically. What this translates into is that if people are saying nasty things to you, you can ignore them and walk away.

Signed,

Diana

Dear Diana,

What does the expression "Finders, keepers; losers, weepers" mean?

Signed,

Curious

Dear Curious,

Let's say you find a 10-dollar bill in the park and there is nobody around to claim it. It's yours to keep. Whoever lost it is probably crying and wishing that they'd been more careful. You found it … and get to keep it.

Signed,

Diana

Dear Diana,

What does the expression "I'll have to sleep on it" mean?

Signed,

Sleep Person

Dear Sleep Person,

It means "I'll have to think about it for a few days." For instance, a mother thinks that the growing family needs to move into a bigger house, but the father isn't sure that they can afford it. So, he says, "I'll have to sleep on it," meaning that he needs time to think about this before making such a big decision.

Signed,

Diana

"Sleeping on It."

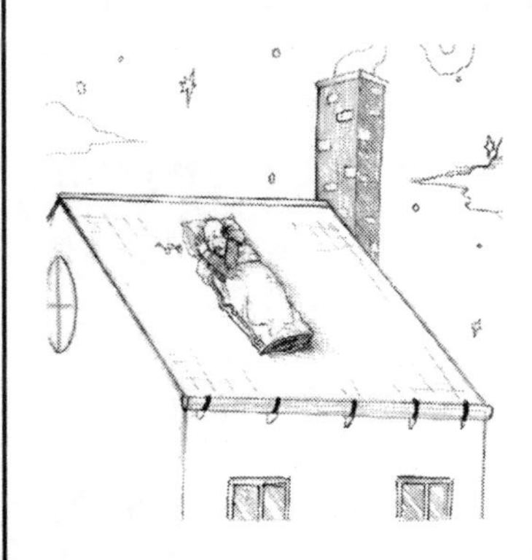

The expression "sleeping on it" doesn't really mean that one is sleeping on anything, like the roof of a building.

It means to give someone a chance to think about something. The person above is thinking about something for 3 days! He is "sleeping on it!"

Dear Diana,

What does the expression "Let's get this show on the road" mean?

Signed,

Road Person

Dear Road Person,

In the old days, traveling circuses and other shows were going from town to town in vans and wagons, and that's where the expression comes from. Now the term is used to mean "Let's get going." For example, you and your mom are cooking dinner for guests, and it's a big job. So she says, "Let's get this show on the road so we can get ready in time."

"Hit the road" means the same thing. If people say that they want to "hit the road," they mean that they want to get going.

Signed,

Diana

Dear Diana,

What does the expression "Two wrongs don't make a right" mean?

Signed,

Wrong/Right Person

Dear Wrong/Right Person,

Here is an example: Tommy hits Billy in the nose. Billy now hits Tommy in the nose. So now they both have bloody noses as a result. Tommy was angry at Billy for taking his math calculator without asking. So, for revenge, he hit him. Billy's revenge for being hit in the nose was hitting Tommy back. "Two wrongs (hitting) don't make a right (solve the situation)."

Signed,

Diana

Chapter 5: Stress Management

Many things in life cause stress. Here are some examples:

1. ***When summer vacation ends and it's time to go back to school.***
2. ***When you are assigned a new teacher or counselor.***
3. ***Knowing that you have to go to the doctor for a shot or procedure or to the dentist to have a cavity filled.***
4. ***Major changes in life, such as moving, a new job, or the death of somebody close to you.***
5. ***Having to finish a project/task within a certain time period.***

It is important to find ways to cope with stress as it can otherwise build and negatively affect both your mental and physical health.

Dear Diana,

I'm going to start a new job next week and I'm freaked out: I can't eat, can't sleep, and can't concentrate. What's going on with me and my body?

Signed,

Freaked-Out Fran

Dear Fran,

You're experiencing a physical and mental reaction to stress. Stress can make you feel tightness in the chest and can cause headaches and chills. It can also affect your appetite.

Many people eat when they are stressed even if they are not hungry. Others don't eat when they are stressed, even though they may be hungry. Stress can also cause loss of sleep and difficulty concentrating.

Here are some solutions for dealing with stress:

1. Listen to relaxing music.
2. Take a hot bath.
3. Take a nap.
4. Go for a walk.
5. Count your blessings.
6. Drink warm milk.
7. Drink cold water.
8. Put a damp cloth on your forehead.

Besides, once you start your new job and get used to it, you most likely won't feel so stressed out.

Signed,

Diana

⌘

Dear Diana,

When I was enjoying a relaxing dinner with a friend the other night, she called me a slow-poke for taking my time eating. We started arguing, which wasn't good because we were in a public place, but I was mad and stomped out of the restaurant. I'm really angry over this and can't get it out of my mind. What can I do to calm down?

Signed,

Unhappy Ursula

Dear Ursula,

It sounds to me like you overreacted. The situation did not call for such anger. If you're about to lose your temper, go to your room or some place where you can be alone and close the door so as not to bother or frighten others.

1. You can punch pillows, tug hard on knitting wool, or squeeze towels. If you are outdoors, you can kick balls, but do not throw anything.
2. You can make angry doodles on paper or squeeze bed pillows together.
3. You can bang plastic cups together or angrily throw garbage away in your garbage pail.

While you are blowing off steam in these ways, you're not damaging property or hurting other people or yourself. Here are a few other options for dealing with your anger.

1. Count to 10 or even 100.
2. Go for a walk (it helped Freaked-Out Fran, so maybe it will help you!).
3. Write about your angry feelings. By writing about your anger, you might find that you are no longer angry.
4. Find somebody you trust and discuss your feelings and how to maintain control. If you have a therapist, set up an appointment or at least talk on the phone.

Signed,

Diana

⌘

Dear Diana,

Thank you for your tips about dealing with stress, but I'm not much of a walker and when I tried punching pillows, it didn't help. Do you have any other ways to deal with stress?

Signed,

Ursula

Dear Ursula,

Another good way to deal with stress is by meditating. Try this:

1. Lie or sit back on a bed or in a chair.
2. Listen to relaxing music.
3. Take long, deep relaxing breaths.
4. Close your eyes.
5. Try to think only positive thoughts. If a bad thought creeps in, bounce it away like bouncing a ball away or pretend it is a helium-filled balloon. In your mind, let go of your balloon so that it and your stress can float way up and away.

I'm sure you'll find that your stress will be gone after a while.

Signed,

Diana

⌘

Dear Diana,

Lunch break at work is at noon. But the other day I was so hungry that I got out my sandwich and started to eat it at 11:30 even though I was supposed to be working. My boss came by and pointed out that I was not following the rules. I'm upset because I didn't follow the rules and because my boss pointed this out to me. What can I do?

Signed,

Hungry Harry

Dear Harry,

It is important to always follow the rules when you are at work. If you don't, someone is going to speak to you about it. It's your boss or manager's responsibility to make sure that you don't goof. By reminding you, your boss is giving you a chance to correct your mistake and get you back on the right track. Apologize and say that it won't happen again. Once you have done this, don't ruminate or perseverate about it. Such a misstep does not mean that you are incapable of doing your job or that you're going to lose your job. It also doesn't mean that you should lose your confidence or sense of accomplishment. You have fixed the problem, so move on and continue to do your job well. When you do this, your stress will disappear!

Signed,

Diana

Balancing Your Life

Try to maintain a good balance between (a) going out and doing things and (b) having some time for yourself. Too much of either one is usually not good. Make friends, get a job, and participate in group activities, but save time for yourself to do errands and chores and to relax. If you spend too much time alone in your apartment, you might end up eating and sleeping too much, watching too much TV, and even thinking negative thoughts. If a good friend calls wanting to get together with you just as you are headed out to do something, you can always ask the friend to join you.

Dear Diana,

I have my reasons for wanting to be alone. One of them is that I don't like getting into issues with people. Another is that I can do lots of things for myself. Nevertheless, I sometimes get tired of being alone. What should I do?

Signed,

Cassie

Dear Cassie,

I suggest trying to maintain a balance between being alone and being with others. Most people need time for themselves but also want to be with their friends. I'm sure that you can find the best balance for yourself.

Signed,

Diana

Managing Your Free Time

Your free time is the time when you don't have to go to your job or a volunteer activity. You can use your free time to schedule appointments with doctors and other health professionals. Your free time is also the time when you can run errands, do chores, pay bills, and make important phone calls. If you have any free time left over after having done all of these things, that is a good time to get together with friends or engage in leisure activities such as knitting, jigsaw puzzles, artwork, crossword puzzles, word-search, sewing, latch hooking, card games, board games, and more! Keep busy. Find something that you love to do in your spare time instead of just sitting on the couch being bored, feeling miserable, overeating or oversleeping.

Dear Diana,

I don't know what has gotten into me all of a sudden. I was busy working on my computer, when all of a sudden, due to a computer glitch, all my work began to erase. Boy, was I mad! At that very moment, my boyfriend, John, phoned wanting to get together. Although I wasn't angry with him at all, I wound up being rude to him and hanging up on him because I was so upset about my computer. How do I make up with him?

Signed,

Christina

Dear Christina,

I understand exactly how you feel. Computer glitches are very annoying. What you need to do is, first, take some long, deep breaths and try to calm down. Second, before you start all over again with your work, phone John and apologize. Politely say, "John, I'm sorry I was so rude to you over the phone. I didn't mean to hurt your feelings. I was just so angry over my computer problem. I didn't mean to take it out on you. I hope you can understand and will forgive me. I'm so sorry." After you have apologized to John, you will feel better and, hopefully, he'll understand.

Signed,

Diana

⌘

Dear Diana,

Can you help me, please? I have a speech impairment. When I'm stressed or have a lot on my mind, I talk quickly and end up stuttering. Then people suggest that I slow down and try to speak more smoothly and fluently, and that makes it all even worse. Part of me dreads being told by others what to do. What can I do?

Signed,

Person With a Speech Impairment

Dear Person With a Speech Impairment,

The advice that you were given – to speak more slowly – is good, but, of course, it isn't that easy, and most people don't understand that. Some people will tease you, but others will be patient until you get the words out. You can usually tell the difference between people who are trying to help and people who are trying to hurt. In the case of those who are trying to help, remember that they mean well and that what they are suggesting may be helpful.

Good luck!

Signed,

Diana

⌘

Dear Diana,

Sometimes I take tranquilizers to help me stay calm when I get overly anxious. But people warn me that tranquilizers can be habit-forming and cause unhealthy side effects. What should I do?

Signed,

Tranquilizer Person

Dear Tranquilizer Person,

You are right that tranquilizers can be habit-forming and should only be used according to your doctor's directions. If you feel that you have become dependent on tranquilizers, talk to your doctor.

Good luck!

Signed,

Diana

⌘

Dear Diana,

Help! I just had a bad dream about being late for work and losing my job as a result. I'm awake now. But what can I do?

Signed,

Worried Waking Up

Dear Worried Waking Up,

Don't worry; it was a dream. Try to forget about it, and whatever you do, don't let it make you late for work in real life.

Signed,

Diana

⌘

It's never too early or too late
To take the time to meditate.

Go for a nice walk,
And share your feelings as you talk.

Always see the bright side of things
And feel the happiness that it brings
Instead of throwing a hissy fit
No one likes that – not one little bit.

Count nice and slowly one to ten,
And you may also count again.

These are things that you can do
To make life much better for you.

Chapter 6:
Taking Charge, Managing Priorities, and Problem Solving

Once you are living on your own, situations will inevitably come up when you will have to decide the best way to proceed. This will include taking charge, deciding on priorities, and solving problems of various kinds. This chapter is full of examples that will help you. Besides, never hesitate to ask for help from your parents, counselors, and other trusted adults.

Dear Diana,

My best friend Audrey and I were helping our group bake some Thanksgiving pies to sell. Suddenly, our Benefits Coordinator, Sheila, came in and told Audrey that she wanted to see her about her benefits the next day. Audrey said she had to work, so Sheila suggested that they discuss the matter right away. But Audrey said, "I can't right now, Sheila. I'm in the middle of helping my group bake pies. Can't we meet in your office when we are done?" Unfortunately, Sheila said that they were not able to wait but that it wouldn't take long.

Hearing this conversation, and seeing how upset she was, I suggested to Audrey that she follow Sheila's instructions to meet her right away, and she did. Do you think I did the right thing by getting involved?

Signed,

Marina

Dear Marina,

It seems to me that you did the right thing. Audrey is your best friend and, therefore, wouldn't mind you getting involved. In other situations, it would not have been appropriate to butt in. I'm glad that you were able to help Audrey, your best friend.

Signed,

Diana

⌘

Dear Diana,

I have an important private meeting scheduled in my apartment with my parents and counselors, but I have a date with my out-of-town friend, Carly, on the same day. What can I do?

Signed,

Sandy

Dear Sandy,

You need to phone Carly and let her know that something urgent has come up. I'm sure she'll understand. You don't have to tell her what that other plan is, but be sure to apologize to her for the disappointment she may feel in having to reschedule your date.

Signed,

Diana

⌘

Dear Diana,

My dad is in town for a meeting, and tonight we're going to meet up so that he can treat me to dinner at my favorite restaurant. Afterwards we are going over a few things in my apartment. But now my counselor wants to see me in her office at 6:30 p.m. What can I do?

Signed,

Kelly

Dear Kelly,

See if your counselor can meet you tomorrow instead. If not, call your dad and explain the situation. Maybe he can meet you in your counselor's office or have dinner a little later.

Signed,

Diana

⌘

Dear Diana,

My retired boss recently passed away in a nursing home. I had been visiting him there for a while and would like to keep going there, because I enjoy meeting the other elderly folks. Is this appropriate?

Signed,

James

Dear James,

Since you were originally visiting your boss and he has now passed away, check with the staff at the nursing home to make sure that it is alright to visit the other folks.

Signed,

Diana

⌘

Dear Diana,

My husband, Dick, and I were planning to go out for pizza with our friend Susan. We were going to leave our baby with my mother, but she just called to say that something has come up and she cannot babysit. What do you suggest we do?

Signed,

Cindy

Dear Cindy,

Call Susan and explain the situation. Then see if she can get a ride to your place. You can order pizza for home delivery and enjoy it at your house while the baby is sleeping.

Signed,

Diana

⌘

Dear Diana,

When I drop off and pick up my daughter Kathy at the station when she comes home to visit, I sometimes park in a tow-away zone because all the parking spaces are taken. Is there a better way of dealing with this situation so that I don't risk my car being towed?

Signed,

Mrs. Jones

Dear Mrs. Jones,

It's never a good idea to park in a tow-away zone, even for a few minutes. Next time, arrange with Kathy to meet you at a pickup point so that you don't have to park the car in a tow-away zone and risk being towed. Another solution would be for you and Kathy to be in touch by cell phone. That way you don't have to leave the car and she can come directly to where you are temporarily parked.

Signed,

Diana

⌘

Dear Diana,

The cover for my mailbox in our apartment complex is missing. Anybody can reach in and take my mail. What should I do?

Signed,

Karen

Dear Karen,

Talk to the property management about getting a replacement cover as soon as possible.

Signed,

Diana

⌘

Dear Diana,

I am recharging my phone's batteries, but I'm getting kind of tired since it's late at night. I have been advised that if you leave the batteries charging overnight, they could get overcharged and it could damage the phone. What should I do?

Signed,

Battery Charger

Dear Battery Charger,

It is true that your phone can be damaged if you overcharge the batteries. When you're ready to go to sleep, unplug the recharger and then plug it in first thing in the morning to finish charging it. Next time you need to recharge the batteries, start earlier in the evening. While your batteries are recharging, you could work on your computer, watch TV, do a puzzle or something else. That way, your batteries will be recharged by the time you're ready to go to bed and you won't have wasted any time.

Good luck!

Signed,

Diana

⌘

Dear Diana,

My parents are coming to pick me up on Thanksgiving Day to go visit our relatives. I plan to pack my suitcase well in advance so I'll be ready, but at the same time, I want to be sure I have enough clothes to wear before going away. What would you suggest?

Signed,

Anxious to Pack

Dear Anxious to Pack,

The first thing is to do your laundry so that all your clothes are clean. Then you should have enough clothes so that you can pack the ones that you want to take and still have clothes left for the days before the trip.

Signed,

Diana

⌘

Dear Diana,

I just heard on the radio that there has been a bad accident on the highway that I take to work. I'm concerned this will cause a delay so I'll be late to work. What should I do?

Signed,

Mike

Dear Mike,

Do you know any other routes to take to work? If not, then call work before leaving home to let them know that you may be late. Don't use your phone while driving.

Signed,

Diana

⌘

Dear Diana,

I'm having a problem with my husband, John. I leave for work earlier than he does and always have to remind him to unplug the coffee maker before he goes to work. The other day he forgot but was able to call a neighbor who has a key to our apartment and ask if she could go over and unplug the coffee maker. Luckily, she was home. But this is not the neighbor's responsibility. John promises me he'll never forget again, but he probably will. What should we do?

Signed,

Kathy

Dear Kathy,

Boy, was John lucky that the neighbor was home! There are several things you can do. For example, you could put up a big reminder sign by the coffee maker, but if I were you, I would buy a coffee machine that turns off automatically after two hours.

Signed,

Diana

⌘

Dear Diana,

What time of day do you think is the best time to go grocery shopping at the supermarket?

Signed,

Food Shopper

Dear Food Shopper,

Don't go food shopping when you're hungry because then you tend to buy more food than if you were not. Also, if possible, do your shopping during the day or in the evening when the store is not so busy. If you go at night, be very careful in a dark parking lot.

Signed,

Diana

⌘

Dear Diana,

Every other weekend I go to my grandparents' house. It is a real drag for me having to carry so much stuff back and forth every time. What can I do?

Signed,

Mary

Dear Mary,

I suggest leaving en extra set of clothes, pajamas, toothbrush, and toiletries at your grandparents'. This way, you will have basic items that you need both at home and at your grandparents', making it easier when you go back and forth. You can either do laundry at your grandma's or ask her to do it for you before you come back next time.

Signed,

Diana

⌘

Dear Diana,

I'm short on money but I have a date with my friend Barbara, who is going to meet me at Charlie's Restaurant after we get off work. What should I do?

Signed,

Catherine

Dear Catherine,

If you're short of money, you shouldn't be going out to dinner. Explain the situation to Barbara. She might offer to treat you; if she does, be prepared to treat her next time. By the way, as we discussed in Chapter 1, you should always have a little money set aside for emergencies, such as a new medicine that the doctor has prescribed that you hadn't budgeted for. Don't spend that on dinner dates.

Signed,

Diana

⌘

Dear Diana,

I just woke up. It's 6:00 a.m., and it's still dark out. They're predicting snow. I'm wondering if I should go to work?

Signed,

Reliable Ted

Dear Ted,

Turn on the news and the weather channel and continue to get ready in case you have to go to work. If you work for a large company, there may be an announcement on the news about whether or not they're open for business. If you take public transportation, listen to the radio or check the local or toll-free number or the website to see if your bus or train is running. If things are on schedule, by the time you're ready to leave for work, you should go. If the weather gets really bad during the day while you're at work, your boss may let you go home early. In that case, go straight home!

Signed,

Diana

⌘

By now, I hope you are catching the idea of idiomatic expressions – never take them literally. Here are some more.

Dear Diana,

What does the expression "A watched pot never boils" mean?

Signed,

Pot Watcher

Dear Pot Watcher,

If you keep watching a pot on the stove waiting for it to boil, it seems to take longer than expected. Of course, it actually doesn't, but the meaning of this expression is that if you're just waiting for something to happen, it will seem to take much longer than if you do something else while waiting. For example, if you're doing a load of wash at the laundromat and you just sit there and watch it, it will seem to take forever. If you have something to read or a friend to talk to, it will take just as long, but it won't seem that way.

Signed,

Diana

Dear Diana,

What does the expression "carried away" mean?

Signed,

Carried Away Inquirer

Dear Carried Away Inquirer,

It means that you are so focused on something that you can't do or think of anything else at the moment. For example, suppose somebody is doing a word-search puzzle and is enjoying it to the point where she doesn't want to stop, even to eat dinner.

Signed,

Diana

Dear Diana,

What do the expressions "Oh, you're telling me!," "Oh, you bet!" and "Oh, you can say that again!" all mean?

Signed,

Oh! Inquirer

Dear Oh! Inquirer,

All of those idiomatic expressions have to do with agreeing with somebody about something. Here are some examples:

John: "My gosh! It sure is windy today!" Mary: "Yes. You're telling me!" (She agrees with John that it's very windy; it sure is!) Somebody is struggling to open a stuck door, telling somebody else, "This door sure could use a fixing." The other person responds, agreeing, "Oh, you can say that again." Sara: "What a lovely day!" Tom: "You bet!" (He means he agrees with her completely.)

Signed,

Diana

Dear Diana,

Every now and then, my mother tells me, "Don't bring that up." But we've only got one floor and there's no basement to bring things up from. So I have absolutely no idea what she's talking about.

Signed,

Bring Up Inquirer

Dear Bring Up Inquirer,

This has absolutely nothing to do with carrying something up from somewhere. It means being selective about what you talk about. For example, perhaps your mother has told you that Cousin Joe is getting a divorce but that it is not appropriate to discuss at Thanksgiving dinner. She might say, "When you see Cousin Joe, don't bring that up."

Signed,

Diana

Dear Diana,

What does the expression "the bottom line" mean? I don't get it.

Signed,

Bottom Line Inquirer

Dear Bottom Line Inquirer,

The expression comes from financial statements where the last line (the bottom line) is the most important because it shows the balance – how much money you have. So we use the expression to mean the main point and the most important thing.

Here's an example: You are trying to cook dinner and also deal with a phone call when all of a sudden, the doorbell rings and the dog starts to bark. You clearly have too many things happening at once and you have to choose which is the most important to focus on. In this case, your bottom line is to make sure you don't leave stuff unattended on the stove, even if it means that you have to get off the phone and ignore the doorbell and the dog.

Signed,

Diana

Dear Diana,

How can I babysit for two children after school and still have time to do my chores and homework before dinner?

Signed,

Kathy

Dear Kathy,

You can't. Your priorities are to do your chores and homework. If you need all the time before dinner to do your chores and homework, you won't be able to babysit.

Signed,

Diana

⌘

Dear Diana,

I just came home from work and am tired. How can I deal with my laundry and my dinner?

Signed,

Steve

Dear Steve,

Do your laundry first. Otherwise you will have no clean clothes for work tomorrow. While your clothes are washing, make yourself a quick and simple meal. For example, a sandwich and soup from a can. That way you can get to bed early and rest up for the next day.

Signed,

Diana

P.S. Another option is to try allowing time for doing chores before going off to work. Good luck!

⌘

Dear Diana,

I have a pizza date tonight with my best friend Laurie, but she just mentioned that she has a doctor's appointment at 4:00 and I have a counselor's appointment at 6:00. In between we each have to do our chores. What can I do?

Signed,

Norma

Dear Norma,

Have pizza with Laurie at 7:00 or reschedule.

Signed,

Diana

⌘

Dear Diana,

I have an appointment with my therapist next Wednesday at 1:30. My friend Julie is expecting me to travel-train her on the same day. What can I do?

Signed,

Vicky

Dear Vicky,

Your appointment with your therapist is most important. Tell Julie you will travel-train her some other day.

Signed,

Diana

⌘

Dear Diana,

I'm often late for my job and other scheduled appointments because I get busy in the morning doing my laundry and other chores. What can I do?

Signed,

Kathy

Dear Kathy,

If you want to do your laundry and other chores before work, you must get up earlier in order to allow more time to do them. If this is difficult for you, do those things when you get home. Always know what time you must be out the door in the morning to get to work on time, and never let laundry or other chores interfere with that.

Signed,

Diana

⌘

Dear Diana,

I didn't have time to make my bed this morning. As soon as I got home, I got busy with my computer and I didn't do it then either. Now, it's late in the day. I'm tired and my bed is still not made up. What can I do?

Signed,

Carol

Dear Carol,

Frankly, some people never make their beds. But this can get pretty sloppy and be embarrassing when somebody comes to see you. I suggest that as a rule you make up your bed in the morning. There will be days when you don't have time to make up your bed in the morning. In those cases, make sure to make it up as soon as you get home before doing anything else.

Signed,

Diana

⌘

Dear Diana,

While waiting for my ride this morning, I decided to make my lunch. I forgot to keep an eye out for my ride, and missed it. How can I avoid that in the future?

Signed,

John

Dear John,

Either allow more time to make your lunch (get up earlier) or make your lunch the night before. You can also set a timer to go off to remind you of when your ride is coming.

Signed,

Diana

⌘

Dear Diana,

After seeing my therapist, I have to be at home waiting for the maintenance people, but I might want to do a few errands on the way home. How can I deal with all of this in one day?

Signed,

Gretchen

Dear Gretchen,

The important thing is to be home for the maintenance people, so do your errands later or the next day.

Signed,

Diana

⌘

Dear Diana,

I'm expecting my mother to come by for a mother-daughter date today as we're both off work. She is not coming until 11:15. I would like to do my banking first. The bank is two blocks away from my apartment and it opens at 9. Do you think I'll have enough time?

Signed,

Cindy

Dear Cindy,

Yes, provided you get up in time to get to the bank promptly when it opens. So, don't let yourself be distracted. Get up, get dressed, and get to the bank. Then you'll have plenty of time to do your banking and be ready for your mother-daughter date.

Signed,

Diana

⌘

Dear Diana,

I have to see my dentist today at 2:00 and my counselor at 5:00. But I would still like to drop off a package at the post office and get some tickets at the train station for an upcoming trip. I might not have enough time for all this in one day. What can I do?

Signed,

Janie

Dear Janie,

Your priorities are the dentist and your counselor. The post office and the train station can be done another time.

Signed,

Diana

⌘

More expressions
Are so much fun.
These expressions
Are almost done.

Dear Diana,

My friend Carol told me, "Listen, Barbara, I don't mean to burst your bubble, but flying off on a magic carpet is just fantasy. You can't get to your parents' house by magic carpet. You will either have to take the train or ask one of them to pick you up." But I haven't any bubble to burst. Please explain to me why Carol used that phrase.

Signed,

Barbara

Dear Barbara,

The expression "Burst one's bubble" means to destroy somebody's fantasy. For example, your idea of a magic carpet was a fantasy and Carol "burst your bubble."

Signed,

Diana

Bursting Your Bubble.

"Bursting your bubble" doesn't really mean bursting a bubble blown from bubble gum in your face.

"Bursting your bubble," as shown above, means being very disappointed at not getting what you had so wished for, like a present!

Dear Diana,

When my parents wanted me to be more careful about how I spend my allowance money, they added, "Money doesn't grow on trees." Well, of course not. But what's that got to do with me trying to save money?

Signed,

Mark

Dear Mark,

When people say "Money doesn't grow on trees," they mean "Money isn't that easy to get." You have to work for it and save it. You can't go out and pick dollar bills off the trees, as though they were apples. Too bad! Wouldn't it be nice?

Signed,

Diana

"Money Doesn't Grow on Trees."

This man is collecting leaves, not money. The expression refers to how easy it is to collect leaves, but how much more difficult it is to collect money.

Dear Diana,

I heard an impatient customer in a restaurant call out to the server, "Hey! Step on the gas!" How can the poor server do that when he isn't driving a car? What does "Step on the gas!" mean?

Signed,

Maria

Dear Maria,

When you're driving a car and you put your foot on the gas, the car speeds up, so people use the expression to mean "get moving!" or "hurry up!" in lots of other situations besides driving. In other words, the impatient and rather rude customer in the restaurant wanted the server to hurry up with the food.

Signed,

Diana

Chapter 7:
Safety and Emergencies

General Safety Tips

Safety is very important and involves most aspects of our lives. The following will help you know how to take certain precautions and how to act in an emergency to keep yourself and others around you safe and out of harm's way.

Dear Diana,

My Uncle Luigi works in a deli making sandwiches. At lunch, the shop gets really busy and the staff is kind of crowded in the back as they hurry up to get customers' orders ready. The other day, my uncle was slicing bread and because of the rush, he was careless and nearly cut his finger off. He had to go to the emergency room and now he won't be able to work for several weeks. I'm very concerned about him. When he comes back to work, do you have any helpful advice for him?

Signed,

Laura

Dear Laura,

I think that the main problem here was that your uncle was too rushed. Surely, he knows the safety rules for using knives, but let's go over them for your sake. First of all, you must always remember to cut away from yourself so as not to stab yourself. Keep your fingers away from where the blade is cutting and don't try to work faster than you comfortably can. Pay attention to what you're doing. Never use knives if you are tired, sleepy, or taking a medication that could impair your judgment or coordination. Always remember to carry a knife down by your side and never with the blade up in the air. Never hold a knife by the blade, or pass it with the blade pointing towards another person. When putting knives in the dishwasher, insert them with the blades facing down. Never play with knives. I hope your uncle is better soon.

Signed,

Diana

Special Cards for Special Needs

If you are like most people, you probably carry a lot of cards around, such as your picture ID, your food stamp card, your bus pass, your pharmacy care card, and your emergency card with information about who to call if you are hurt or sick. Keep all these cards in your wallet or a special pocket in your purse so that you know where they are when you need them. If you have a Medicare card or other health insurance card, it's best not to carry those around routinely. Keep them in your lockbox and just take them out when you go to the doctor and then remember to put them back again after the appointment.

Dear Diana,

I was waiting for the bus, all loaded down with my school books when it started to rain really hard. There was no sign of the bus, but this young man who seemed friendly pulled right up to the bus stop in his car and asked me where I lived and whether I would like a lift. I let him drive me home, but when I got home, my mother was very upset with me for getting a lift home. I thought she would be glad that I didn't get soaking wet, but she wasn't. What do you think?

Signed,

Janelle

Dear Janelle,

Your mother had a very good reason to be upset with you. You should never get into a car with a stranger, no matter how hard it is raining or how much stuff you have to carry. A stranger is somebody you don't know. Maybe he seems friendly, but you really have no idea whether he is. He might have wanted to rob, kidnap, or hurt you. Never get into a conversation with a stranger. If a stranger is bothering you and refuses to leave you alone, go into a store and ask the storekeeper to help you contact the police. If you are at home and someone calls you on the telephone and refuses to identify himself, hang up immediately. If somebody who you are not expecting comes to your door, don't open the door.

Signed,

Diana

How to Carry a Purse or Pocket Book

The safest way to carry a pocketbook is around the neck or across your body. If you have it over your shoulder or in your hand, the chances are you could lose it or have it snatched.

Swimming

It's never a good idea to swim when there is no lifeguard. Always go with a buddy. Never swim past the ropes. Don't use floating toys as life-saving devices. Only dive in pools that are deep enough and permit you to dive. If you are next in line to dive, don't start until the person in front of you is out of the way.

Riding in a Car

Never get into a car if you think that the driver has had alcohol to drink. Don't ride with somebody who is using a cell phone, sending text messages, eating a sandwich, fixing their hair, or in any other way not concentrating on the road. Wear a seatbelt at all times. Sit back. Keep your hands, feet, and head inside of the vehicle. As we have already discussed, NEVER RIDE WITH STRANGERS!

Stairs

Never run up or down the stairs. Always use the banister. If you have carpeting on your stairs and it's getting worn, try to get it fixed or replaced.

Fires

Fires can be started by playing with matches. Other fire hazards are old rags that are soaked with grease, oil, or paint, or things hanging over lights. If you smoke in bed and doze off, you could start a fire that might kill you or others. Make sure that you have a smoke alarm and that the batteries are changed at least once a year. If the smoke alarm goes off, get out of your apartment and ask a neighbor to call 911 for you.

Dear Diana,

Last week, while I was in the other room, I smelled smoke coming from the clothes dryer. When I went to look, I saw that something in the dryer was on fire. I called 911, grabbed my keys, and went outside to wait for the fire department. Fortunately, they came pretty fast and put the fire out, but now the dryer is ruined. How could a fire have started in there?

Signed,

Carolina

Dear Carolina,

A fire can start in a dryer if the vent is clogged up with lint. Please be sure to clean the lint out of the vent on a regular basis. Never leave the house with the dryer running. Just imagine what would have happened if you hadn't been home to call the fire department!

Signed,

Diana

⌘

Dear Diana,

The street where I live is a one-way street, but my mother always wants me to look both ways before crossing. Is this really necessary, if the cars are only coming from one direction?

Signed,

Henry

Dear Henry,

Your mother is absolutely right. Always look both ways before crossing any street. Sometimes the drivers disobey the one-way sign. If you need to cross the street, use the crosswalk if there is one and observe the pedestrian-activated lights.

Signed,

Diana

⌘

Dear Diana,

I live in an old building. On my first day in my apartment, I put some toast in the toaster and a mug of water in the microwave to warm it up for tea. Suddenly, all the lights went off in the kitchen. I called the landlord. He said I had blown a fuse and he had to put in a new one. He was kind of annoyed at me, but I don't really understand what happened. What do you think?

Signed,

Horace

Dear Horace,

In old buildings, the electrical wiring may not be sufficient to power all of your electrical appliances at once. Try not to use more than one appliance at a time. For example, first make your toast and then warm up the water for your coffee or tea. If you limit the number of appliances you're using at the same time, you're less likely to blow a fuse or start an electrical fire. Another safety tip about appliances: Never immerse electrical appliances in water. This can cause electric shocks and even death. Also, in the cases of appliances such as toasters or hair dryers, it is always a good idea to unplug them when not in use.

Signed,

Diana

⌘

Dear Diana,

My grandmother lives alone, and my mom's biggest concern is that she might get hurt in the kitchen. My mom checks Grandma's kitchen for safety hazards on a regular basis. It's getting to be a problem, but Grandma refuses to move, so we're stuck with the situation for now. Do you have any thoughts on how we can help keep my grandmother safe?

Signed,

Elena

Dear Elena,

Your mother is absolutely right to be concerned. The kitchen is one of the most hazardous areas in the house no matter how old or young you are. Here are some helpful suggestions for your mother and grandmother, and for everybody else who is using the kitchen:

1. If an overhead light bulb needs to be changed, never try to do this by yourself when you are home alone. Wait for somebody to come and help using a proper stepladder, not a chair.
2. Make sure you have a mop to wipe up spills on the floor before anybody slips and gets hurt.
3. Be careful with the stove and oven. When taking something out of the oven, use potholders, not dishtowels. If you boil water for hot drinks, it's a good idea to use a whistling teakettle so you don't forget to turn off the heat when the water comes to a boil.
4. If you have a gas oven and smell gas in your kitchen, you might have a leak. Don't turn the oven or burners on or strike any matches. Call the gas company immediately to have it checked out.

Signed,

Diana

⌘

Time for more expressions.

Dear Diana,

Our Aunty Susan is kind of bossy, but my mother says that she is a "paper tiger." I don't understand. What does she mean?

Signed,

Niece of a Tiger

Dear Niece of Tiger,

Don't worry; Aunty Susan isn't about to start growling. When we call somebody a paper tiger, we mean that they may seem scary but that they really aren't. If you look at a picture of a tiger, it might look scary until you remember that it's only a picture on a piece of paper.

Signed,

Diana

Dear Diana,

What does the expression "An apple a day keeps the doctor away" mean?

Signed,

Apple Inquirer

Dear Apple Inquirer,

If you eat a healthy diet, including fresh fruits and vegetables, you reduce your risks of getting sick and won't have to go to the doctor. Of course, it's not that simple. Eating an apple every day doesn't prevent you from ever having to go to the doctor. What the expression means is that if you take good care of your health, maybe you won't have to make too many emergency doctor visits.

Signed,

Diana

An Apple a Day Keeps the Doctor Away!

Of course, eating an apple a day doesn't mean that you will never get sick and need to see the doctor. What it does mean is that by eating healthy, it is less likely that you will get sick and have to see the doctor! The person below is happy and healthy because he is eating an apple and other healthy foods.

Dear Diana,

What does it mean "Not to give a hoot" about something?

Signed,

Hoot Inquirer

Dear Hoot Inquirer,

When somebody says that they don't give a hoot about something, it means that they don't care about it.

Signed,

Diana

Dear Diana,

When somebody tells me to "Stick to the point," I don't understand what they mean. Do I need sticky tape? What should I do?

Signed,

Confused

Dear Confused,

You don't need sticky tape to stick to the point! For example, if you and your counselor are talking about vocational skills, this is not the time to start talking about grooming. Stick to, or keep focusing on, the topic at hand. Here's another example: If your friend invites you for a potluck and is about to tell you what to bring, this is not the time to discuss movie dates.

Signed,

Diana

Dear Diana,

What does the expression "It's no use crying over spilled milk" mean?

Signed,

Spilled Milk Inquirer

Dear Spilled Milk Inquirer,

If you spill your milk, you'll have to mop it up and you can't drink it. Crying will not bring it back. We use the expression when something happens that can't be fixed. Here's an example: A little girl is watching a parade, holding her mother's hand in one hand and a helium balloon in the other. The girl lets the balloon go, and it rises out of sight. Her mother tells her, "I'm so sorry. The balloon was filled with helium and we can't get it back. Maybe we can get another one. Meanwhile, it's no use crying over spilled milk."

Signed,

Diana

Dear Diana,

What does the expression "Time flies when you're having fun" mean?

Signed,

Flying Time Inquirer

Dear Flying Time Inquirer,

The expression means that time seems to go faster than usual when you are enjoying what you're doing. If you're not having fun or are not very busy, time sometimes seems to drag. Of course, time doesn't speed up or slow down depending on whether or not you are enjoying what you're doing. It just seems like that.

Signed,

Diana

911 Emergencies

When you pick up the phone and call 911, you will be connected to the fire department, police, and ambulance service. If you call on your landline, they will automatically know where you are. If you call from your mobile phone, you will have to tell them where you are. Once you have made the call, they will respond immediately. So this must never be done as a practical joke.

Dear Diana,

Hi, it's Carolina again. Remember me? I'm the one who had a fire that started in my clothes dryer, As I already wrote to you, when that happened, I grabbed my keys and also stopped to call 911 before I got out. My mother is always reminding me not to forget my keys when I go out, so I can get back in. But this time she said I did the wrong thing. Can you explain?

Signed,

Carolina

Dear Carolina,

Your mother was right, because this was an emergency, which could have threatened your life. If you are at home and something catches on fire, GET OUT IMMEDIATELY, even if you have to leave behind your keys, cell phone, pocketbook, etc.! The reason I advise this is that a fire can spread very rapidly, and in the few minutes you take to find your keys, the fire may grow so big that you won't be able to get out. Once you do get out, go to a neighbor and ask them to call 911 for you.

Signed,

Diana

⌘

Dear Diana,

I was coming home late from work. By the time I got off the bus, it was already dark. I was a little scared, but I had my umbrella with me, so I figured that if somebody tried to steal my purse, I would hit them with my umbrella. Fortunately, I got home safe, but I want to know what you would do if you were in that situation.

Signed,

Millie

Dear Millie,

Your plan to defend yourself with an umbrella is a bad one. If somebody is threatening you with a gun or knife for your bag, HAND IT OVER! There is nothing in your bag that cannot be replaced. DO NOT TRY TO FIGHT BACK, because if you get the attacker angry or agitated, he may injure you. With any luck, once you hand over your bag, he will run away. You then should go into the nearest store or business and ask them for help in calling the police.

Signed,

Diana

⌘

Dear Diana,

I'm confused about when I should be calling 911. The other day, my roommate had a headache and a sore throat. Should I have called an ambulance or 911?

Signed,

Tom

Dear Tom,

No, you should not call an ambulance or 911 for a headache or a sore throat. You should call 911 only for major emergencies, such as chest pains or difficulty breathing. If the person becomes unresponsive, call 911 immediately, because she might be having a heart attack or a seizure. Stay with the person until the ambulance comes. The same rules would apply if somebody has fallen off a ladder or been hit by a car and seems to be seriously injured.

Signed,

Diana

Non-911 Emergencies

There are all kinds of emergencies. Non-911 emergencies are emergencies in which you don't need to call 911, but you will still need to do something to take care of an urgent problem. Examples include an appliance that doesn't work or makes a strange sound, a leaky basement, a power failure, or having to see one of your doctors or therapists for an issue that is not life-threatening.

Dear Diana,

My clothes washer has sprung a leak. Is this a 911 emergency?

Signed,

Maria

Dear Maria,

No, this is not a 911 emergency, but you do have to do something. Shut the machine off and don't use it until it's fixed. You will need to call an appliance repair service for this problem. Meanwhile, you can take your clothes to the laundromat. If you have good friends, you might ask them if you can do you laundry at their place.

Good luck!

Signed,

Diana

⌘

Dear Diana,

I'm feeling very anxious and would like to see my therapist, Dr. Tom Jones, but my next appointment is not until a month from now. What can I do?

Signed,

Harry

Dear Harry,

Call Dr. Jones today and tell him how you're feeling. Ask him for an appointment as soon as possible or at least a chance to talk for a few minutes on the phone.

Good luck!

Signed,

Diana

⌘

Dear Diana,

The last time I lost electrical power, I was still living with my parents, but now I have a place of my own. This morning, I lost power, but it came back in an hour, so I didn't do anything. But what should I do if the power goes off and doesn't come back right away? Who should I call?

Signed,

Doris

Dear Doris,

Your first call should be to whoever supplies your power. The phone number is on the bill you get from the power company. Let them know where you live. They will tell you approximately when you will get your power back. If you live in an apartment building and the entire building has no power, you can check with a neighbor and if somebody else has already called, then you don't have to. You may consider this a 911 emergency but it isn't. DO NOT CALL 911 just because you have no power. Only call 911 if you need the police, the fire department, or an ambulance.

Signed,

Diana

⌘

Dear Diana,

There is a storm coming, and on the radio they keep telling people to be prepared. What exactly should I do?

Signed,

Neil

Dear Neil,

Always have a few flashlights handy and be sure that you know where they are – you'll have trouble finding them in the dark. If a storm is predicted overnight, it's a good idea to have a flashlight by your bed so that you are not stumbling around in the dark. It's also a good idea to have a transistor radio so you can get news even if you have no power. Usually, your landline will still work during a power outage and so will your cell phone, until the battery runs down. So, you can use your phones to call for help. Make sure ahead of time that you have batteries for your flashlights and radio. It is also a good idea to have a few bottles of water on hand and some food that doesn't need to be refrigerated. If the power outage goes on for several days, see if you can find a friend who has power and go over there for a little while.

Signed,

Diana

My book is almost at an end,
But more expressions I will send.
Goodbye, good luck,
Enjoy your skills.
Independent living
Brings many great thrills.

⌘

Dear Diana,

What does the expression "Turning over a new leaf" mean?

Signed,

New Leaf

Dear New Leaf,

That expression means you're starting over again in an effort to improve the situation. For example, after having smoked for 20 years, somebody decides that she's not going to smoke any more. That person is turning over a new leaf. When people decide to make New Year's Resolutions that involve self-improvement, such as not eating too much junk food or allocating more time to do their chores before going off to work for the day, they are also turning over a new leaf.

Signed,

Diana

Dear Diana,

What does the expression "You're pulling my leg" mean?

Signed,

Confused

Dear Confused,

That means you're teasing or kidding somebody. You're not literally pulling their leg. For instance, sometimes when somebody asks me where my roommate is, I tease them by saying she's "in my pocket." I am pulling their leg. I am teasing.

Signed,

Diana

Dear Diana,

What does the expression "Your mother doesn't work here. Please pick up after yourself" mean?

Signed,

Janice

Dear Janice,

That sign is sometimes posted in offices. As a child at home, when you make a mess, your mother usually cleans it up, but as a grownup, it is your responsibility to clean up after yourself.

Signed,

Diana

Dear Diana,

What does the expression "A penny saved is a penny earned" mean?

Signed,

Penny

Dear Penny,

This is an expression that emphasizes the value of saving money. The idea is that saving money is a way of also earning money.

Signed,

Diana

Dear Diana,

When I criticized a classmate for being late for class, our teacher told me "People who live in glass houses shouldn't throw stones." That's true, because it could break the glass, but what does it have to do with my pointing out that my classmate was late?

Signed,

David

Dear David,

The expression means that you should not criticize others for making the same mistakes you do. So perhaps you are often late for class.

Signed,

Diana

Dear Diana,

In geography class, I got a lot of the answers right, but I was really just guessing and the teacher knew that. So she said I was "Flying by the seat of my pants." What does that mean?

Signed,

Theresa

Dear Theresa,

When we use that expression we mean that the person has done something difficult without the necessary experience or ability. Usually it involves a lot of luck.

Signed,

Diana

Dear Diana,

My friend Peter said that it's "Time to close the book" on Fred since he's already had enough time to apologize to us. But why must we close the book on him? What does that mean?

Signed,

Mike

Dear Mike,

"To close the book" on somebody means to declare that a matter involving them is finished.

Signed,

Diana

Index

Index of Expressions

Related Books

Learning the Hidden Curriculum:

The Odyssey of One Autistic Adult

by Judy Endow, MSW;
foreword by Brenda Smith Myles, PhD

Drawing from her personal experiences, Judy Endow provides lots of hidden curriculum items that pertain to most areas of adult life. In relating how she personally has learned to more successfully maneuver social interactions, she also presents a framework for developing the ability to more quickly assess a situation and take steps to avoid making social blunders BEFORE they have been committed. A sampling of strategies includes Pause and Match, Laugh Along, Recognize and Expand Black-and-White Thinking, and It Is Not Necessary to Report All My Truths. Judy's framework enables readers to learn to create their own social "rules" and, as a result, live freer, more successful lives. The fact that this book is written by an autistic person who has learned by trial and error makes it all the more valuable.

ISBN 9781934575932 | Code 9077 | Price: $21.00

Becoming Remarkably Able

Walking the Path to Talents, Interests, and Personal Growth

by Jackie Marquette, PhD

This much-needed resource helps youth with all levels of ASD identify their gifts and strengths. The model leads youth into active community involvement during the transition to adulthood and provides emotional support throughout the process. With a focus on increased capability and independence, the workbook-style guide helps establish goals and paths to pursue in the quest for self-value and a quality of life beyond high school.

ISBN 9781934575017 | Code 9992 | Price: $22.00

From AAPC Publishing

The Hidden Curriculum of Getting and Keeping a Job:

Navigating the Social Landscape of Employment: A Guide for Individuals With Autism Spectrum and Other Social-Cognitive Challenges

by Brenda Smith, Myles, PhD, Judy Endow, MSW, and Malcolm Mayfield, BS Civil Eng

Adults on the spectrum often have difficulties getting and keeping a job that are unrelated to their job skills. This practical and easy-to-use book provides necessary yet often untaught information on a variety of topics related to getting a job, finding a mentor, networking, using agencies, interviewing, talking with supervisors, dealing with on-the-job-frustrations, understanding the social rules at work and many others. Authored by two individuals on the spectrum who have extensive experience in helping others become employed, Judy Endow and Malcolm Mayfield, as well as Brenda Smith Myles, an internationally known writer and speaker on autism spectrum disorders.

ISBN 9781937473020 | Code 9078 | Price: $20.00

To order these or other related books, go to www. aapcpublishing.net

P.O. Box 23173
Shawnee Mission, Kansas 66283-0173
www.aapcpublishing.net

CPSIA information can be obtained at www.ICGtesting.com
Printed in the USA
LVOW07s0503110914

403400LV00006B/6/P